The 15 Titles of God Hidden in the Lord's Prayer

DR. MAXWELL UBAH

The 15 Titles of God Hidden in the Lord's Prayer

Copyright © 2022 by Dr. Maxwell Ubah.

Ebook ISBN: 978-1-63812-466-5
Paperback: ISBN: 978-1-63812-465-8

All rights reserved. No part in this book may be produced and transmitted in any form or by any means, electronic, or mechanical, including photocopying, recording, or by any information storage and retrieval system, without permission in writing from the copyright owner.

The views expressed in this work are solely those of the author and do not necessarily reflect the views of the publisher hereby disclaims any responsibility for them.
Published by Pen Culture Solutions 10/19/2022

Pen Culture Solutions
1-888-727-7204 (USA)
1-800-950-458 (Australia)
support@penculturesolutions.com

CONTENTS

Foreword.. i

Introduction... iii

1: Father... 1
1.2: I Will Be God to You... 7
1.3: From God to Father... 11
1.4: Our Father, the Hidden Mystery of Adoption........ 15
1.5: Father, in the Name of Jesus............................... 19

2: Exalted One... 23
2.2: The Lord of the Heavens.................................... 27

3: King.. 31
3.2: The Titles of Our King....................................... 35
3.3: Miracles and the Kingdom Concept................... 37

4: Lord and Master.. 39
4.2: Sons and Servants... 43
4.3: Not as I Will.. 49
4.4: Complete Obedience Required.......................... 55

5: Provider.. 57
5.2: Jehovah-Jireh... 61
5.3: Can God Prepare a Table in the Wilderness?....... 67
5.4: Is God against Prosperity?................................. 71

6: Healer... 75
6.2: Does God Still Heal Today?............................... 79
6.3: How Many Will God Heal?............................... 81

7: Holy God.. 83
7.2: Everything about God Is Holy........................... 87

8: Merciful God 89
8.2: Completely Forgiven 93
8.3: Come Boldly to Obtain Forgiveness 99
8.4: Apply the Blood 101

9: Restorer of Broken Relationships 103
9.2: The Cost of Failing to Forgive 105

10: Guide and Leader 111
10.2: How God Leads 115
10.3: Cooperating with God's Leading 117

11: Strong Deliverer 121
11.2: Four Accounts of Deliverance 125

12: Our Protector 131
12.2: Psalm 91: A Covenant of Protection 133

13: All-Powerful God 139
13.2: All Power Comes from God 143

14: Glorious One 147
14.2: Power and Glory: Two Sides of the Same Coin ... 151

15: Eternal God 155

About the Author 157

FOREWORD

On first contact with this book, a feeling of nostalgia runs through your spine as you remember scores of pupils reciting the Lord's Prayer to start their day in school. You must have also heard the Lord's Prayer recited and chanted several times to close one service or another in the church. Indeed, every believer must have encountered the Lord's Prayer at one time or another in his or her Christian walk.

Dr Maxwell, in his new book *The 15 Titles of God Hidden in the Lord's Prayer*, pushes back the boundaries and reveals the depth and wealth of this prayer beyond the normal church liturgy. He delves into the protocol required for accessing the presence of God, reveals the beauty of fellowship with the Father, and x-rays the benefits we derive when we dare go into His presence. The book further underscores the truth that God is just a breath away and that if only we dare to pray, we will soon realize that all we need is available through God.

Jesus, in His response to His disciples in Matthew 6:9–13, taught the Lord's Prayer as a guide to effective prayer as opposed to the "showmanship" that was reminiscent of His days. The point Jesus was making was that it is not about praying but is rather all about praying *right*. If praying was vitally important in the ministry of Jesus, then this generation cannot afford to pray less.

Every believer must understand that although nothing happens without the grace of God, we cannot abandon the place of prayers. Prayers have always been and will ever remain pivotal in our relationship with God. We cannot outgrow prayers; nor can we ever do without them. Dr Maxwell, in this book, has done justice to the subject matter of our Lord's Prayer, looking at it from so many angles.

I recommend this book as a must-read for every Christian. Don't keep this truth to yourself; read it and pass it round to everyone around you. Recommend it to others.

Maranatha!

Dr. Mike Okonkwo
The Bishop of TREM

INTRODUCTION

You can connect with someone in an instant, but intimacy—real intimacy—takes time to develop. To develop intimacy with someone, you need to trust that person with the essence of who you are—to become unmasked and remove the veil of your facade and let them into the world of your dreams, hopes, fears, and even your deepest struggles. The more we get to know people at that level, the more intimate we are with them. But getting to know someone that way takes time and effort.

Developing intimacy with God also takes time. We need to prod beyond superficial knowledge and understanding into the deep things of God. On our part, getting intimate with God takes *desire*—the hunger to want to know God—and *dedicated pursuit* to seek God above all else, just as the deer pants for the water brooks (Psalm 42:1). When God sees both attributes in us, He peels back the layers and takes us deeper in getting to know Him. He honours us with His presence as we diligently seek Him (Hebrews 11:6).

Sometimes, however, God pursues intimacy with us and reveals Himself to us even when we are not intentionally seeking Him, just as He revealed Himself to Abraham in Mesopotamia (Acts 7:2), Moses at the burning bush (Exodus 3:1–6), and Saul on his way to Damascus (Acts 9:1–5). At such times, we cannot lay claim to our desires, dedicated pursuits, or even our holiness as the source of the revelation (see Acts 3:12); we recognize that we are simply products of mercy and grace and that God chose to reveal Himself to us in spite of us not seeking Him. (Hosea 2:14, Jeremiah 31:3).

That is how the message of this book came about; God chose to reveal the essence of the message without any input from me. It didn't come from my thinking it through or studying hard about it; it came by grace. At the beginning of 2017, I took my church through a series on prayers based on the Lord's Prayer when God, in His infinite mercies, opened my eyes to see the hidden nature of His character in the verses in the Lord's Prayer. Guess what? The revelation came after I had finished the series! God began where I stopped! As the good Lord peeled back the layers of the verses to show me His hidden nature and attributes, all I could say was, "Wow! Thank you, Lord, for your mercy and grace."

I saw many titles of God in the Lord's Prayer, but they can all be grouped into fifteen major titles using keywords and phrases. Each title could be the subject of a book, and some books have been written about some of the titles herein. I was tempted to explore each title in much more detail, but that would mean writing fifteen different books instead of one. Instead, I decided to keep it concise and straightforward to give you, my readers, a quick insight into the nature and character of God in the Lord's Prayer as revealed to me by Jesus Christ through His Spirit. Feel free to build on them and share them with your family and friends, and preach them to your members if you are a pastor. You don't need my permission to preach or teach it. Just go ahead and be a blessing to others.

In this book, you will see God as:

- Father—"*Our Father*"
- Exalted One—"*in heaven*"
- King—"*Your kingdom come*"
- Lord and Master—"*Your will be done*"
- Provider—"*give us this day our daily bread*"
- Healer—"*give us this day our daily bread*"
- Holy One—"*and forgive our debts*"
- Merciful God—"*and forgive our debts*"
- Restorer of Broken Relationships—"*as we forgive our debtors*"

- Guide and Leader—"*and do not lead us into temptation*"
- Strong Deliverer—"*deliver us from evil*"
- Protector—"*deliver us from evil*"
- All-powerful God—"*for Yours is the power*"
- Glorious God—"*and the glory*"
- Eternal God—"*forever*"

I wrote this book with one goal in mind: to help you develop a greater level of intimacy with God. My prayer is that as you read this book, God will open your eyes to see Him in a new way. May each new revelation of God help you develop a deeper level of intimacy with Him. Like the men on the road to Emmaus, may your hearts not only burn as you read this book, but may they also be opened to see the risen Lord (Luke 24:32–35).

To emphasize certain scriptural truths, I have used italics, bold typefaces, and capital letters.

God bless you.

Max

The Lord's Prayer

Matthew 6:9–13

⁹ In this manner, therefore, pray:
Our Father in heaven,
Hallowed b e Your name.
¹⁰ Your kingdom come.
Your will be done on earth as it is in heaven.
¹¹ Give us this day our daily bread.
¹² And forgive us our debts,
As we forgive our debtors.
¹³ And do not lead us into temptation,
But deliver us from the evil one.
For Yours is the kingdom and the power and the glory forever.
Amen.

1

Father

*Reference in the Lord's Prayer: **"Our Father."***

When Jesus taught His disciples to pray, He asked them to begin with "Our Father". He revealed not only the first title of God in the Lord's Prayer but also the nature and essence of God.

Real prayer begins with knowing God as Father. Jesus didn't ask us to pray to a distant or imaginary being; He asked us to pray to "Our Father".

I believe "Father", the first revelation of God in the Lord's Prayer, reveals the very essence of who God is: The God who was, and is, and always will be a Father.

Our God is our Father, the God who had always wanted a family and a fatherly relationship with His children. Isaiah calls Him "the Everlasting Father":

Isaiah 9:6
[6] For unto us a Child is born, unto us a Son is given; and the government will be upon His shoulder. And His name will be called Wonderful, Counsellor, Mighty God, EVERLASTING FATHER, Prince of Peace.

One of the names of God given here is "Everlasting Father", meaning that God is the Eternal Father—the God who before the onset of time (eternity past) was a Father and who after the expiration of time (eternity future) will remain a Father. "Everlasting" means that before God (Elohim) created the heavens and the earth in Genesis 1:1, He was a Father. That is, the title "Everlasting Father" preceded that of Elohim, the Creator of the heavens and the earth.

I believe the Father-heart of God, His desire for a relationship with humanity, is the reason for the creation of the heavens and the earth. Remove God's Fatherly love, and creation has no meaning or purpose, for the purpose of every created thing is revealed only through understanding His heart towards us.

The Father-heart of God was the reason for the creation of the first man.

Psalm 8:3–5
3 When I consider Your heavens, the work of Your fingers, the moon and the stars, which You have ordained,

4 What is man that you are mindful of him, and the Son of Man that you visit him?

5 For You have made him a little lower than the angels, and You have crowned him with glory and honour.

Man holds a special place not only in creation but also in God's heart. David couldn't understand the place man held in God's heart that he queried, "What is man that you are mindful of him, and the Son of Man that you visit him?" He literally said, "Why do You bother so much about man? What is it about man that Your love cannot let go?"

Genesis 1:26 gives us the clue: "Then God said, *'Let Us make man in Our image, according to Our likeness*; let them have dominion over the fish of the sea, over the birds of the air, and over the cattle, over all the earth and over every creeping thing that creeps on the earth.'"

Man is the only being who was created in the image of God. In that phrase "in the image of God," we see that God was willing to share His essence with man. I believe on the basis of this phrase that God deposited His DNA in man. Why do I say so? Consider Genesis 5:1, 3:

Genesis 5:1, 3
¹ This is the book of the genealogy of Adam. In the day that God created man, *He made him in the likeness of God.*
³ And Adam lived one hundred and thirty years and begot a son *in his own likeness, after his image*, and named him Seth.

If you read these verses carefully in conjunction with Genesis 1:26, you will notice that Adam's creation by God is described in the same wording ("in the likeness [of]") that is used of Seth's birth by Adam.

Genesis 1:26
²⁶ Then God said, "**Let Us make man in Our image, according to Our likeness**; let them have dominion over the fish of the sea, over the birds of the air, and over the cattle, over all the earth and over every creeping thing that creeps on the earth."

Genesis 5:1, 3
³ And Adam lived one hundred and thirty years and **begot a son in his own likeness, after his image**, and named him Seth.

So, what God did in creating Adam was exactly what Adam did in begetting Seth. Seth was born in the likeness of Adam, after his image, just as Adam was created in the likeness of God, after God's image.

The word "created" is used for Adam, and "begot" for Seth, but the process is the same; both were made after the likeness of another, in the image of another person. Consequently, we can assume that with Adam's creation, God begot Adam.

Therefore, Adam was God's firstborn and the beginning of the human race. In Adam, we see a glimpse of God's eternal heart, the Father-heart. And if Adam passed his DNA and genes to Seth, then God must have passed His DNA and genes to Adam.

So why did God create man in His image? He did so to have fellowship with man as a father has fellowship with his children. Now you understand why man was the only being in creation that God regularly came down to have fellowship with (Psalm 8:4).

Adam was the firstborn of the human race made in the image of God to fellowship with God in a Father–son relationship.

Real prayer, as prescribed by Jesus, begins with knowing God as Father. The "Father" concept means that Christianity is based on family—a family between God and His children made possible by Jesus Christ.

When we understand that prayer is a family affair, there would be no need for high-sounding words and gimmicks. Prayer should be as easy and natural to us as breathing, because we are speaking to our Father!

Matthew 6:5–6
⁵ And when you pray, you shall not be like the hypocrites. FOR THEY LOVE TO PRAY standing in the synagogues and on the corners of the streets, THAT THEY MAY BE SEEN BY MEN. Assuredly, I say to you, they have their reward.
⁶ But you, when you pray, go into your room, and when you have shut your door, *pray to your Father who is in the secret place;* and your Father who sees in secret will reward you openly.

The Pharisees missed the essence of prayer: prayer is speaking to our Father; it is not an activity we do to be seen by men. And when you speak to your father, you do not use vain or highfalutin words: "And when you pray, do not use vain repetitions as the heathen do. For they think that they will be heard for their many words" (Matthew 6:7).

I would like to repeat here again that "Our Father" means Christianity is a family concept. The family concept runs throughout the Scriptures but is present especially in the New Testament epistles.

Ephesians 2:19
¹⁹ Now, therefore, you are no longer strangers and foreigners, but fellow citizens with the saints and members of the household of God.

Ephesians 3:14-15
¹⁴ For this reason I bow my knees to the Father of our Lord Jesus Christ, ¹⁵ from whom the **whole family** in heaven and earth is named.

God is our Father, and heaven operates under a family structure. Paul wrote to the Ephesian church that *we are members of the household of God*. We are not just citizens of the kingdom of heaven; we are members of the household of God as sons and daughters of our heavenly Father (John 1:12, 1 John 3:1). We are not strangers and foreigners or visitors; we are members of the household of God. We have a right to the privileges of the household.

Did you observe that in Ephesians 3:14, Paul noted that the whole family [of God] in heaven and earth is named? There is a family of God in heaven made up of saints who have gone yonder, and there is a family of God on earth made up of those who are washed by the blood of the Lamb but are yet to be translated. However, irrespective of the location, the whole family in heaven and earth is named. Your name is written as part of the family of God.

When Jesus asked His disciples to pray beginning with "Our Father", He wanted them to know that they are in the family of God and that God is their Father. It is the first and perhaps the most important revelation of God in our prayer lives.

When we pray, we are speaking to God as our Father!

1.2

I Will Be God to You

To appreciate the title "Father", the first revelation of God in the Lord's Prayer, we need to step back and see how God chose to reveal Himself in different dispensations.

In Genesis 1:1, God revealed Himself as the Creator with the title "Elohim".

In Elohim, God is the God of all His creation: angels, animals, man, the solar system, the sea, and so on. Everything He created was signed off by Elohim. Elohim is about ownership. God owns everything.

However, in Genesis 1:26, God revealed Himself as a Father in the creation of man and woman, as we have established. God's eternal plan has always been a Father–son relationship with humanity.

What is the difference between Elohim and Father?

As Elohim, all created beings can call Him God; as Father, only those created *in His image* are members of His family. This is akin to the difference between the president of a nation and the father of someone's child. Everyone can call that individual Mr. President, but not everyone can call him Father. Only his child can call him that.

When Adam sinned and lost the privilege of the Father–son relationship, God did not abandon His eternal plan. He made a promise of redemption through the seed of the woman (Genesis 3:15) but chose to begin the redemptive process with Abraham.

In His dealings with Abraham, we see His eternal plans for humanity. Take, for example, the promise He covenanted with Abraham in Genesis 17:7: "And I will establish My covenant between Me and you and your descendants after you in their generations, for an everlasting covenant, **to be God to you** and your descendants after you."

In this verse, God moved from Elohim, the Creator of the heavens and the earth, to Abraham's personal God. He was no longer just the Creator to Abraham; He was now Abraham's personal God.

There are four insights in this covenant promise:

God initiated it: Abraham didn't ask for or initiate it. God decided to become Abraham's personal God. This is grace, pure and simple.

It is an everlasting covenant: God irrevocably committed Himself to Abraham and his descendants for all eternity. This is the reason why He is called the God of Abraham.

It is exclusive: No individual can lay claim to God as his personal God unless he is one of Abraham's descendants either by birth or through adoption.

It is the first account of adoption: God adopted Abraham as His first family on earth. This made Abraham God's adopted child and the beginning of God's plan of adoption for the human race, a plan that culminated in the coming of Jesus Christ. You now understand why Jesus is called the son of Abraham (Matthew 1:1) and the seed of Abraham (Galatians 3:16), and we too are called the seed of Abraham in Christ and heirs according to the promise because of this covenant promise (Galatians 3:29).

This promise brought Abraham into an intimate relationship with God. God knew Abraham, and can I say, Abraham knew God. When Abraham called, God had to answer because Abraham held a special place in His heart: "And the Scripture was fulfilled which says, 'Abraham believed God, and it was accounted to him for righteousness'. *And He was called the friend of God"* (James 2:23).

Abraham moved from being an ordinary individual to being heaven's representative on earth, the friend of God. What can be stronger than God binding Himself "to be God to you and your descendants after you"?

1.3

From God to Father

We have seen how God moved from being the Creator of the heavens and the earth to becoming Abraham and his descendants' personal God. That is one reason the Jews are so successful. They have won more Nobel prizes than any other race in the world; they have patented more inventions than all the Arab countries put together, and they have never lost a major battle when they cooperated with God, all because God promised Abraham to be God to him and his descendants after him.

In that promise, God adopted Abraham and his descendants as the first family on earth. That promise was the beginning of God's eternal redemptive plan for humanity and the fulfilment of His Father-heart.

When God asked Moses to bring the children of Israel out of Egypt, He said to Pharaoh through Moses, "*Israel is My son, My firstborn*" (Exodus 4:22). In that message, we see three things:

God is the Eternal Father of the nation of Israel through the covenant promise to Abraham,

Israel is the first nation in God's prophetic calendar, and

Israel will point the way to God and be the channel through which God will adopt other nations.

In this message, we see the Father-heart of God, the God who wanted a family, and a Father–son relationship with the nation of Israel, though they did not fully appreciate it. And all through the Old Testament Scriptures, we see glimpses of His Father-heart. When He made a covenant with David, He revealed Himself as a Father:

2 Samuel 7:12–14

¹² When your days are fulfilled and you rest with your fathers, I will set up your seed after you, who will come from your body, and I will establish his kingdom.

¹³ He shall build a house for my name, and I will establish the throne of his kingdom forever.

¹⁴ *I WILL BE HIS FATHER, AND HE SHALL BE MY SON.* If he commits iniquity, I will chasten him with the rod of men and with the blows of the sons of men.

In Psalm 103:13, the psalmist recorded God's dealings with our sins in the context of a father with his son. "As a father pities his children, so the Lord pities those who fear Him."

This is repeated in Proverbs 3:12: "For whom the Lord loves He corrects, just as a father the son in whom he delights."

In Jeremiah 31:9, God reminds them that He is "a Father to Israel".

You now understand that the title "Father" is not a New Testament revelation. God had always wanted a Father-son relationship with His children, but they did not get it. They did not use that title. They couldn't conceive of God as Father. No one dared to address Him as Father, call Him Father, or worship Him as Father until Jesus came. In fact, when Jesus called God His Father, they accused Him of blasphemy and wanted to kill Him.

John 5:17–18

¹⁷ But Jesus answered them, "My Father has been working until now, and I have been working."

¹⁸ Therefore the Jews sought all the more to kill Him, because He not only broke the Sabbath, but ALSO SAID THAT GOD WAS HIS FATHER, MAKING HIMSELF EQUAL WITH GOD.

Why did they want to kill him for calling God His Father? Because calling God His Father meant that He was equal with God or in the same class with God. It was too far-fetched for them to use for the Creator of the heavens and the earth. They could not imagine God as their Father. As God the Creator, *yes*. As Father? Not possible. The title Father reveals personal intimacy with God which they could not conceive in their minds.

Jesus came to reveal God as the Everlasting Father, His original title before the creation of the heavens and earth. That's the reason why He asked us to pray starting with "Our Father".

1.4
Our Father, the Hidden Mystery of Adoption

Jesus did not just tell His disciples to start with "Father" or "my Father". He specifically said, "Our Father". I checked twenty-seven different translations of the Lord's Prayer according to Matthew's account, and they all start with "Our Father". It cannot be a coincidence.

"Our" is a collective pronoun. So, what did Jesus have in mind when He said, "Our Father"? In the collective pronoun "our" we see the hidden mystery of our adoption. What do I mean?

"Our" added before "Father" gives us insight into how God became a Father to us and who made it possible.

When man sinned, he lost access to the life of God and became a legal child of the devil. For God to bring humanity back into fellowship with Him, He had to pay the price of our adoption. That is the reason He gave Jesus up for us.

Isaiah 9:6
For unto us a Child is born, unto us a Son is given; and the government will be upon His shoulder. And His name will be called Wonderful, Counsellor, Mighty God, EVERLASTING FATHER, Prince of Peace.

Jesus came as the revelation of the Everlasting Father to restore us into God's family. He came to pay the price of our adoption. Ephesians 1:5 says that God "predestined us to adoption as sons by Jesus Christ to Himself, according to the good pleasure of His will."

Jesus is our ransom; He signed our adoption papers on behalf of the Everlasting Father with His blood, and because of Him, we can call God Father.

So, the "Our" that Jesus added to "Father" literally means "*because of and together with Jesus.*" Anytime we say, "Our Father," we are recognizing the role of Jesus and our relationship with God through Him, for without Him we have no access or right to the Father (John 14:6).

Because of Jesus, God is now our Father. We see the confirmation in John 20:17. When Jesus rose from the dead and Mary Magdalene wanted to cling to Him, His immediate response was, "Do not cling to Me, for I have not yet ascended to My Father; but go to My brethren and say to them, 'I am ascending to My Father and your Father, and *to* My God and your God.'"

There are four truths in this verse.
First, God is the Father of Jesus. He is God's Eternal Son: "I have not yet ascended to *My Father.*"

Second, we are His brothers: "*But go to My brethren.*" Curiously, He didn't call His followers disciples here. They are now His brothers. Why? *I believe the goal of true discipleship is an understanding of sonship*. First, He called them disciples when He chose them; next He called them friends after they had been with Him for a while (John 15:5). But after His resurrection, He called them brothers.

We see this confirmation in Hebrews 2:11: "For both He who sanctifies and those who are being sanctified are all of one, *for which reason He is not ashamed to call them brethren.*"

Jesus is not ashamed to call us brothers. We are the brothers and sisters of Jesus. By calling us brothers, He elevated our position to royalty, higher than that of the angels.

Third, He is also our Father. Jesus moves from "My Father" to "*My Father and your Father.*" Initially it was "My Father," His exclusive right. But after He called them brethren, it became "*My Father and your Father.*" "Just as He is My Father", Jesus said, "He is also your Father", which makes Him "Our Father." Hallelujah. God is no more a Father to Jesus than He is to us.

We have the same legal rights to the Father as Jesus did on earth. Jesus is God's firstborn among many brothers (Romans 8:29). Anytime you use the firstborn title, it means there are other members of the family—other children. Before Jesus' resurrection, He was the only begotten Son (John 3:16). After His resurrection, God now has a lot of sons and daughters, all because of what He did. We are begotten of God and are the brothers and sisters of Jesus. He is the firstborn among many brothers. He is our Lord and big brother!

Finally, Jesus calls Him God: *My God and your God.* Jesus reversed the equation. To the average person, He is God first. To us He is our Father first, and then our God.

The word "Our" that Jesus added makes us joint possessors or claimants to the title "Father" with Jesus. It simply means that our standing before the Father is not inferior to the one Jesus had before the Father when He was on earth. And if the Father heard Jesus always, "Our Father" will hear us always. Praise the Lord!

1.5

Our Father, in the Name of Jesus

Some people teach that the Lord's Prayer is not a New Testament prayer because it is not in the name of Jesus. Such people reveal their lack of understanding of the Scriptures. We have seen that our ability to say "Our Father" is based on Jesus' redemption and resurrection. Every time we say, "Our Father," we are invoking the name of Jesus because we know that Jesus is the only reason we can call God our Father. "But as many, as received Him [Jesus], to them He [Jesus] gave the right to become children of God, to those who believe in His name" (John 1:12).

The title "Our Father" also means that there is not a man or woman on earth that has a better standing before God than you. They might have a better understanding of their rights before the Father or a deeper understanding of their privileges, but they do not have a better standing before God. If you have the same standing with Jesus in "Our Father", you have the same standing as any bishop, apostle, or prophet.

What we enjoy of God is a function of our understanding, not our standing with God. Our standing as children of our Father is the same, but our understanding of our rights is in degrees. And our ability to enjoy our privileges is based on our understanding of our rights. This is the reason Paul prayed for the Ephesian Church that their eyes of understanding might be enlightened to know the riches of God's inheritance in them (Ephesians 1:17–18). The inheritance is the same for everyone, but it takes light, wisdom, and understanding to enjoy our privileges in God, our Father.

Although we all have the same legal status and the same privileges before our Father, only those who understand their place with the Father will enjoy the benefits of the relationship.

Can you pause for a moment to meditate and worship your Father? Thank God for Jesus and the privileges of calling God, your Father. You can worship the Father where you are, right now, in your heart.

The woman by the well missed the issue. It is not about a place to worship but about whom we worship.

John 4:21–24
[21] Jesus said to her, "Woman, believe me, the hour is coming when you will neither on this mountain nor in Jerusalem, *worship the Father*.
[22] You worship what you do not know; *we know what we worship*, for salvation is of the Jews.
[23] But the hour is coming, and now is, when the true worshipers will worship the Father in spirit and truth; *for the Father is seeking such to worship him*.
[24] God is Spirit, and those who worship Him must worship in spirit and truth."

Worship is more than a place; it is a relationship with a person—our Father.

Worship is more than words; it is the state of your heart—a grateful heart saved and washed by the blood of Jesus.

Worship is a Father-son relationship made possible by the blood of Jesus.

Real worship is intimacy with the Father that begins with "Abba, Father."

Romans 8:15
¹⁵ For you did not receive the spirit of bondage again to fear, but you received the Spirit of adoption by whom we cry out, "Abba, Father."

Galatians 4:6
⁶ And because you are sons, God has sent forth the Spirit of His Son into your hearts, crying out, "Abba, Father!"

The Father is seeking people who have been washed by the blood of Jesus, people who understand His true worth to worship Him as Father, crying out from their hearts, "Abba, Father!"

2

The Exalted One

Reference in the Lord's Prayer: **"in heaven."**

Location matters. Sometimes just by knowing where someone lives, you have an idea of who that person is.

Buckingham Palace? The monarchy in England.

The White House? The president of the United States of America.

Aso Rock? The president of the Federal Republic of Nigeria.

When Jesus asked the disciples to pray, He asked them to say, "Our Father *in heaven*".

The phrase "*in heaven*" tells us where our Father dwells and, by implication, who He is.

Because He is in heaven, He is unlike any other creature. He is not bound by time and space like the inhabitants of the earth. And since the heavens are higher than the earth, our Father is the Exalted One, the High and Lofty One. No White House, Aso Rock, or Buckingham Palace is as exalted as "in heaven".

Our finite minds cannot truly fathom how exalted our Father is. He is exalted beyond comprehension and above any imaginable limits.

Isaiah 57:15

For thus says THE HIGH AND LOFTY ONE who inhabits eternity, whose name is Holy: "**I dwell in the high and holy place. . .**"

His Person

"In heaven" reveals the magnificence of our Father. The Scriptures inform us that God's throne is in the heavens and the earth is His footstool (Isaiah 66:1). Imagine how great our Father is that He straddles the heavens and the earth just by sitting down. What would happen if He were to stand up? The whole universe would not contain Him! That's who our Father is.

His Power

Our Father stands alone and unrivalled by any other creature in the greatness of His power.

Isaiah 40:12, 15, 18, 22

[12] Who has *measured the waters in the hollow of His hand, measured heaven with a span* and calculated the dust of the earth in a measure? *Weighed the mountains in scales and the hills in a balance?*

[15] Behold, the nations are as a drop in a bucket, and are counted as the small dust on the scales; look, He lifts up the isles as a very little thing.

[18] *To whom then will you liken God?* Or what likeness will you compare to Him?

[22] It is He who sits above the circle of the earth, and its inhabitants are like grasshoppers, *who stretches out the heavens like a curtain*, and spreads them out like a tent to dwell in.

Our Father is so great that He measures the waters or seas in the hollow of His hand. Imagine someone who can hold all the waters of the seas in the hollow of His hand. We see the vastness of the oceans and the ferociousness of the waves of the sea, but to our Father, they are measured in the hollow of His hand. Amazing!

Not only that, but He measures heaven with His span. My mind cannot fathom it. Your span is the distance between the tips of your thumb and your little finger in an outstretched position, and our Father measures heaven with His span. That is, the whole of the stratosphere can fit within His span. Wow!

Or is it the greatness of His power that He weighs the mountains in scales or the hills in a balance? Or is it with His knowledge that He can calculate the dust of the earth? I could go on, but by now you have an idea of how great your Father, God, is.

He is the Exalted One!

Isaiah 40:25–26
25 "To whom then will you liken me, or to whom shall I be equal?" says the Holy One.
26 Lift up your eyes on high, and see who has created these things, Who brings out their host by number; He calls them all by name, by the greatness of His might and the strength of His power; not one is missing.

2.2

The Lord of the Heavens

Reference in the Lord's Prayer: **"in heaven"**

I believe that when Jesus said, "Our Father in heaven", He had something else in mind. Literally, "Our Father in heaven" can be rewritten as "Our Father, who alone lives in heaven". Only our Father can lay claim to heaven as His home. Heaven is not only His dwelling place and residence but His property. He is the sole owner. All others are guests and visitors.

Deuteronomy 10:14
Indeed heaven and *the highest heavens belong to the LORD your God*, also the earth with all that is in it.

Heaven and the highest heavens belong to the LORD. There is no argument about it. . There is no dispute about ownership. No other being can lay claim to the highest heavens. It is God's right for all eternity.

Lucifer tried to lay claim to the highest heavens, and he failed woefully.

Isaiah 14:12–15
[12] How you are fallen from heaven, O Lucifer, son of the morning! How you are cut down to the ground, you who weakened the nations!
[13] *For you have said in your heart: 'I will ascend into heaven*, I will exalt my throne above the stars of God; I will also sit on the mount of the congregation on the farthest sides of the north;

¹⁴ I will ascend above the heights of the clouds, *I will be like the Most High.*'

¹⁵ *Yet you shall be brought down to Sheol, to the lowest depths of the Pit.*

The highest heavens belong to the Lord.

Our Father is unlike any created being. He stands alone and exalted in His person, position, and power. Lucifer was not content to remain in his position and tried to ascend to the highest heavens to sit there, to be like the Most High. The consequence? He fell and became the devil, the accuser of the brethren.

God, our Father, is the Lord of the heavens. He will not share that glory with others.

When the sons of men attempted to build a tower that would reach the heavens, God confused their language (Genesis 11: 4-7). Why? The highest heavens belong to God.

I believe there is a hidden message here. In Ephesians 6:12, Paul writes that our battle in spiritual warfare is "against principalities, against powers, against the rulers of the darkness of this age, against spiritual hosts of wickedness *in the heavenly places.*"

The forces we wrestle with are in the heavenly places, and our Father, who dwells in the highest heavens, is the Lord of the heavens. This means that we are wrestling from a position of strength and victory.

Our Father is the Lord of the heavens. The forces arrayed against us are not as powerful as our heavenly Father, who daily watches over us. We are sons and daughters of the Lord of the heavens, and in that knowledge, we shall overcome all the forces of darkness arrayed against us.

Isn't it comforting to know that our Father is the Lord of the heavens and that it doesn't matter what the spirits in the heavenly places arrayed against us, as we shall overcome? For if God, our Father, is for us, who shall be against us? (Romans 8:31).

3

King

Reference in the Lord's Prayer: **"Your kingdom come."**

When Jesus taught His disciples to pray, "*Your kingdom come*", He revealed another hidden title of God, our Father: He is the King of the Universe!

You cannot talk about a kingdom without a king, for a kingdom is the domain of a king. Remove a king and what you have is a republic.

Jesus established the fact that heaven operates under a kingdom concept; it is not a democracy. In a kingdom, you don't elect your leaders; you accept them.

Heaven operates under a monarchical system and our Father is King. He is the Sovereign Ruler of the universe, the Governor among the nations (Psalm 22:28). There is no rotational presidency in God's kingdom because our Father is King forever. He wasn't voted in. Therefore, He cannot be voted out.

1 Timothy 1:17
[17] Now to the KING ETERNAL, IMMORTAL, INVISIBLE, to God who alone is wise, is honour and glory forever and ever. Amen.

Until the earth comes under the kingdom system of God, peace will forever be elusive.

Many Scriptures point to God, our Father, as King. We might not be able to exhaust these Scriptures here, but let's consider some.

One of the very first pictures of God as a King is seen in Exodus 15:18. In their victory song over Egypt and Pharaoh, Moses sang, "The Lord shall reign forever and ever." The word "reign" comes from the Hebrew word "*mālak*", which means "to ascend a throne, exercise the functions of a king or queen; to be set up as a king."

Here we see Moses describing God as King over the earth, and He shall reign forever and ever.

When Balak hired Balaam to curse the Israelites, Balaam revealed God as King in one of his prophecies:

Numbers 23:21
[21] He has not observed iniquity in Jacob, nor has He seen wickedness in Israel. The LORD his God is with him, AND THE SHOUT OF A KING is among them.

The shout of a King is among them! Israel was a kingdom with God as their King. Now you understand why God's heart was pained when they asked for a king like the other nations. They did not understand that God was their King, and they rejected His Kingship over them (1 Samuel 8:4–7).

Our Father is a king! Psalm 47 beautifully captures the reign of God as King:

Psalm 47
[1] Oh, clap your hands, all you people! Shout to God with the voice of triumph!

² For the Lord Most High *is* awesome; **He is a great King over all the earth**.

³ *He will subdue the peoples under us*, and the nations under our feet.
⁴ *He will choose our inheritance for us*, the excellence of Jacob whom He loves. *Selah*
⁵ God has gone up with a shout, the Lord with the sound of a trumpet.
⁶ Sing praises to God, sing praises! **Sing praises to our King**, sing praises!
⁷ **For God *is* the King of all the earth**; sing praises with understanding.
⁸ God reigns over the nations; God sits on His holy throne.
⁹ The princes of the people have gathered together, the people of the God of Abraham. **For the shields of the earth *belong* to God**; He is greatly exalted.

This psalm describes God as the King over all the earth! He is not just King over the heavens but also King over the earth. When Jesus asked us to pray that His Kingdom comes on earth as it is in heaven, that was what He had in mind. Psalm 47:9 NIV captures the concept, "The nobles of the nations assemble as the people of the God of Abraham, **for the kings of the earth belong to God**; he is greatly exalted."

Some other references to God as King include the following:

The Lord sat enthroned at the flood, and *the Lord sits as King forever.* (Psalm 29:10)

They have seen Your procession, O God, the procession of my God, *my King*, into the sanctuary. (Psalm 68:24)

For *God is my King from of old*, working salvation in the midst of the earth. (Psalm 74:12)

"But cursed be the deceiver who has in his flock a male, and takes a vow, but sacrifices to the Lord what is blemished—*for I am a great King*," says the Lord of hosts, "And my name is to be feared among the nations." (Malachi 1:14)

3.2

The Titles of Our King

The Scriptures describe God's Kingship in specific ways:

Great King over the earth (Psalm 47:2).
King of glory (Psalm 24:7).
King from of old (Psalm 74:12).
King above all gods (Psalm 95:3).
A great King (Malachi 1:14).
King of Israel (John 1:49).
King of the Jews (John 19:3, 19).
King of righteousness (Hebrews 7:2).
King of peace (Hebrews 7:2).
King of kings (1 Timothy 6:15; Revelation 17:14; 19:16).
King eternal (1 Timothy 1:17; Psalm 29:10).
King immortal (1 Timothy 1:17).
King invisible (1 Timothy 1:17).
King of the saints (Revelation 15:3).

3.3

Miracles and the Kingdom Concept

The most profound message of the New Testament is the message about the kingdom of God. Jesus spent all His time preaching about the coming kingdom.

Matthew 4:17
¹⁷ From that time Jesus began to preach and to say, "Repent, for *the kingdom of heaven* is at hand."

The message of God's kingdom is the message of God's reign, rule, and sovereignty. It is enthroning God's rule over our lives. And everywhere God's kingdom message is preached and accepted, miracles, signs, and wonders are the natural results, for our King cannot coexist with sickness, poverty, demons, and every work of darkness.

Matthew 4:23
²³ And Jesus went about all Galilee, teaching in their synagogues, preaching *the gospel of the kingdom,* and *healing all kinds of sickness and all kinds of disease* among the people.

Healing is a manifestation of the kingdom concept. God and sicknesses cannot cohabit. Where God's kingship is enthroned, sicknesses and diseases are dethroned.

Luke 11:20

²⁰ But *if I cast out demons* with the finger of God, *surely the kingdom of God has come upon you.*

The kingdom of God and the kingdom of darkness are mutually exclusive. You can belong to only one kingdom and have one king over your life. There is no dual citizenship spiritually. Therefore, if God is King over us, the devil has no right to torment or oppress us with anything that is not part of the kingdom of God.

Colossians 1:13

¹³ He has delivered us from the power of darkness and translated us into the kingdom of the Son of His love.

The message of the kingdom of God puts an end to the works of darkness in the lives of men. We need to begin to enthrone God as King over us by praying, "Your kingdom come." When we pray that way, we are asking God to reign over us, to ride majestically into our situations, and to rule in the midst of our enemies.

Psalm 45:3–6

³ Gird Your sword upon Your thigh, O Mighty One, with Your glory and Your majesty.

⁴ And in your Majesty ride prosperously because of truth, humility, and righteousness; and Your right hand shall teach You awesome things.

⁵ Your arrows are sharp in the heart of the king's enemies; the peoples fall under You.

⁶ Your throne, O God, is forever and ever; a sceptre of righteousness is the sceptre of Your kingdom.

Psalm 110:2

² The LORD shall send the rod of Your strength out of Zion. Rule in the midst of your enemies!

4

Lord and Master

Reference in the Lord's Prayer: **"Your will be done."**

When Jesus asked us to pray, "Your will be done", He revealed another hidden title of God, our Father; He is also our Lord and Master!

The title "King" usually goes together with "Lord", as seen in Revelation 19:16, "King of kings and Lord of lords".

God is not just our King; He is also our Lord. As our Lord, He is our Master, and we are His servants. As our Master, His will for our lives is non-negotiable.

Christianity is not just a call to a relationship with God as our Father; it is also a call to obedience, to accept the Lordship of God over our lives.

As Master, God deserves our highest loyalty, fear, and reverence.

Malachi 1:6
⁶ A son honours his father, and a servant his master. IF THEN I AM THE FATHER, where is My honour? AND IF I AM A MASTER, where is My reverence? Says the LORD of hosts to you priests who despise My name. Yet you say, "In what way have we despised Your name?"

Here God describes Himself not only as "The Father" but also as a Master and our Master. As our Master, He is asking, "Where is My reverence?"

God is Our Father and Master! Let us not get used to God as our Father only that we forget that He is also our Lord and Master. Knowing God as Father births gratitude; recognizing Him as our Master births reverence and holy fear.

God deserves our utmost reverence and fear—the type of holy fear that keeps us away from sin. This is the same kind of fear that kept Joseph from sinning with Potiphar's wife when no one was watching and prevented him from maltreating his brothers when he had the power to do so (see Genesis 39:9; 42:18).

Some will be quick to point out that in the New Testament -we should not fear God, that we should only love God. They forget Peter's admonition to believers to: "Honour all people. Love the brotherhood. *Fear God.* Honour the king" (1 Peter 2:17).

In this verse, Peter gives us a manual—a code for successful living:
People—honour
Brotherhood—love
God—fear
King—honour

Peter asked us to *fear God*. It can't be more straightforward than that! He continued in the eighteenth verse, "Servants, *be submissive to your masters with all fear*, not only to the good and gentle but also to the harsh."

The concept of fearing God is about being submissive or obedient to the will of God whether we like it or not.

Since God is not only our Father but also our Master, we need to obey His will whether our flesh feels like it or not. Jesus got to the point at which His flesh felt like pulling back when He prayed, "O My Father if it is possible, let this cup pass from Me." But He understood the concept of submission. He continued, "Nevertheless, not as I will, but as You will" (Matthew 26:39).

This is the meaning of recognizing God as our Master. We no longer live our lives as we want but as He wills.

4.2

Sons and Servants

The average believer knows that God in Christ has made us sons and daughters unto Him; that's why He is our Father in the first place. But they believe that servants are for the Old Testament people. I have received messages from people saying that we are sons, not servants in the New Testament.

Such messages fail to rightly divide the Scriptures (1 Timothy 2:15). Paul, the man who brought us the mystery of redemption and the revelation of our sonship rights, described himself as a "bondservant of Jesus Christ".

Romans 1:1
¹ Paul, *a bondservant* of Jesus Christ, called to be an apostle, separated to the gospel of God.

How can the man who brought the revelation of sonship describe himself as a bondservant? Was he alone? No. Peter, James, Jude, and Timothy all described themselves as bondservants:

Simon Peter, a *bondservant* and apostle of Jesus Christ. (2 Peter 1:1)
Paul and Timothy, *bondservants* of Jesus Christ. (Philippians 1:1)
James, a *bondservant* of God and of the Lord Jesus Christ. (James 1:1)
Jude, a *bondservant* of Jesus Christ, and brother of James. (Jude 1:1)

So, what did Peter, James, Jude, Paul, and Timothy know that many of today's ministers do not know?

Here's the key:
Sonship deals with *our relationship with God as our Father.* Servitude (*servant*) deals with *our relationship to His will and assignment.*

One deals with God's person; the other deals with God's will. We are sons and daughters because Jesus saved us and adopted us into the family of God; we are servants because we are expected to serve God's purpose with our lives.

I want you to consider Paul's and Peter's statements again:

Romans 1:1
¹ Paul, a ***bondservant*** of Jesus Christ, ***called to be an apostle***, separated to the gospel of God.

2 Peter 1:1
¹ Simon Peter, a ***bondservant*** and ***apostle*** of Jesus Christ.

Did you notice that in both instances, the title of "bondservant" is connected to an assignment—the ministry of an apostle? A bondservant (a servant) is someone whose life is bonded, or irreversibly yoked, to the master's will—whether in the capacity of an apostle, a prophet, a pastor, an evangelist, or someone singing or cleaning pews in church!

Has it ever occurred to you that the most common title of Jesus Christ in the Old Testament book of Isaiah is "Servant of Jehovah"? (Isaiah 42:1–6; 52:13–15; 53:1–12; 61:1–3).

Isaiah called Him not only a Son (Isaiah 9:6) but also a Servant. Why? Because He is the Son of God in His essence and His relationship with the Father, but He is the Servant of Jehovah to fulfil the will of God for humanity. He is the first and perfect Son-Servant.

Before Peter, James, Jude, Paul, and Timothy all called themselves bondservants, our Lord was the first servant of Jehovah.

Acts 4:27–30

²⁷ For truly against **Your holy Servant Jesus**, whom You anointed, both Herod and Pontius Pilate, with the Gentiles and the people of Israel, were gathered together

²⁸ To do whatever Your hand and Your purpose determined before to be done.

²⁹ Now, Lord, look on their threats, and grant to Your servants that with all boldness they may speak Your word,

³⁰ by stretching out Your hand to heal, and that signs and wonders may be done through the name of **Your holy Servant Jesus**.

Jesus is God's holy Servant to fullfil the will of the Father for our salvation.

Only servants fulfil the will of their Master. A son enjoys his father's privileges, but a servant bears his master's yoke. And since Jesus asked us to take His yoke upon ourselves (Matthew 11:29), that yoke includes the yoke of service, just as He took the yoke of the Father and humbled himself unto death, fulfilling the Father's will for the salvation of humanity (Philippians 2:5–9).

God needs sons to worship Him, but He needs servants to serve Him and fulfil His purpose. In Malachi, God particularly emphasized the place of the sons who serve Him, whom I call "serving sons."

Malachi 3:16–18

¹⁶ Then those who feared the LORD spoke to one another, and the LORD listened and heard them; so a book of remembrance was written before Him for those who fear the LORD and who meditate on His name.

¹⁷ "They shall be Mine," says the LORD of hosts, "On the day that I make them My jewels. and **I will spare them as a man spares his own son who serves him**."

¹⁸ Then you shall again discern between the righteous and the wicked, between one who serves God and one who does not serve Him.

The most important people in the kingdom are sons and daughters who serve God's purpose with their lives. They are God's jewels, set apart for honour.

Righteousness is a standing we have before God through Christ. However, our standing requires us to serve God in Christ. Then we shall again discern between the righteous and the wicked—between one who serves God and one who does not.

Paul called our service done in righteousness to God "the fruits of righteousness", and he prayed for the Philippian church to be filled with them (Philippians 1:11).

As Christians, we are not saved just to enjoy and claim our rights; we are saved to serve out His purpose, "For we are *His workmanship*, created in Christ Jesus for good works, which God prepared beforehand that we should walk in them" (Ephesians 2:10).

We are workmen or servicemen, not just sons and daughters. As pastors, we have preached sonship to people and taught them how to claim their rights in God; we need also to preach servanthood to them and show them how to fulfil their responsibilities to God and to do works of righteousness. We are not just sons made to enjoy divine privileges; we are servants, too, made to carry out God's eternal plan for our generation.

Every title of God revealed in the Lord's prayer also has a reference to us. If God is our Father, we are His children; if He is exalted, we should humble ourselves before Him; if He is our King, we are citizens of His kingdom; and if He is our Lord, we are His servants.

We are all bondservants, whether to sin or to righteousness. None of us is completely free. We are all servants to something. As Christians, we should be bondservants to righteousness—people who are so in love with our Master that we have willingly given up our rights and personal freedom for the will of our Master and Lord.

Romans 6:18, 22

¹⁸ And having been set free from sin, you became ***slaves of righteousness***.

²² But now having been set free from sin, and having ***become slaves of God***, you have your fruit to holiness, and the end, everlasting life.

We are not just set free from sin; we are slaves of righteousness and slaves of God. We are God's children because we have been set free from sin, but we are God's slaves to produce fruit to holiness, yoked eternally to His will and purpose. We need to preach both messages to our people—that we are the children of God in our relationship with Him but the slaves of God in our responsibilities to Him. There is no relationship without responsibilities, and Christianity is no exception. The difference is that God enables us by His grace to fulfil our responsibilities, but He does not exempt us from them!

Are you just a son, or are you a serving son?

I am writing this book as a serving son. I am using my gift to serve God's purpose for my generation—to be a blessing to someone in His name.

I first wrote the manuscript of this book in 2018 and somehow left it and published another book titled *A Yes God: God's Heart Concerning Your Needs*. In August 2019, I had a stirring in my spirit to complete and release this book. I immediately went to work—service.

That's the attitude of a servant. We say to God our Father and Master, "Here am I; send me" (Isaiah 6:8). We make ourselves available to be used by God to fulfil any purpose He wants to fulfil in our generation, just as David served God's purpose for his generation (Acts 13:36).

My service doesn't define who I am; I am a child of God washed by the blood of Jesus. That's my identity. My service is my gratitude to God for saving me, and my willingness to be used by Him to bless others through me.

Romans 12:1
¹ I beseech you therefore, brethren, by the mercies of God, that you present your bodies a living sacrifice, holy, acceptable to God, *which is* your reasonable service.

Why was Paul begging them, and what was He asking from them? Many of them who are saved do not see the responsibility placed upon them, an expectation from God concerning their lives. They are brethren, or brothers and sisters, washed by the blood of Jesus, but they do not understand that God has a plan for their lives. And that plan can only come to pass as they cooperate with God's purposes by yielding themselves to Him. Their bodies, the instrument for the fulfilment of God's plan, need to be sacrificed to Jehovah as a living sacrifice, a sacrifice done daily. It is their reasonable service.

The same concept applies to us. Our reasonable service is yielding our lives to Jehovah on the altar of sacrifice for the accomplishment of His will.

4.3

Not as I Will

If God is our Lord, then we are His servants. The title "servant", as we have seen, is not derogatory but is a privilege—the privilege of partnering with God for the accomplishment of His purposes in our generation (Acts 13:36; 1 Corinthians 3:9).

Servants do not have a will of their own. Their wills have been subsumed under their master's will. When Jesus said, *"Nevertheless, not as I will, but as You will,"* He revealed this quality of servants. Our lives become the medium for the expression and fulfilment of God's will.

Paul understood this concept. He said in Galatians 2:20, "I am crucified with Christ; *it is no longer I who live, but Christ lives in me*; and the life which I now live in the flesh, I live by faith in the Son of God, who loved me and gave Himself for me."

Any message of grace that doesn't talk about us dying to self is not complete. Paul said, "I am crucified with Christ." I—everything about me: my will, emotions, plans, desires, and all that I am—have been crucified with Christ. It is no longer I who lives, but Christ lives in me. For example, suppose someone offends you. In your flesh, you want to either retaliate or hold malice against the person. But when you remember that you are crucified with Christ and that, on the cross, Jesus asked for forgiveness for those who crucified Him, you allow Christ to live through you and love the person nonetheless.

That's the idea—allowing Christ to live through us and fulfil God's eternal plans for our individual lives.

Our lives are borrowed lives—a lease from God to us for which we would give account (Romans 14:12).

Jeremiah 10:23 NIV
²³ Lord, *I know that people's lives are not their own*; it is not for them to direct their steps.

Wow! We, too, like Jeremiah, need to come to the same understanding—that our lives are not our own. There is nothing like "It's my life" once you become a Christian. Your life is no longer your own. We have been bought with a price (1 Corinthians 6:20). We are not lords unto ourselves; it is not in our power to direct our steps or to determine our future. We are servants, and as servants, we should not trust in our understanding but seek His will for our lives (Proverbs 3:5–6).

As servants, our wills died the day we accepted Jesus as Lord over us. Most times when we ask people to receive Jesus, we tell them to receive Him as their Saviour. But our calling as Christians is not just to accept Jesus as our Saviour; it is also to accept Him as our Lord.

Romans 10:9
⁹ That IF YOU CONFESS WITH YOUR MOUTH THE LORD JESUS and believe in your heart that God has raised Him from the dead, you will be saved.

Did you see it? We confess the Lord Jesus to be saved. Confessing the Lord Jesus is confessing Jesus as Lord. Salvation is about acknowledging the Lordship of Jesus over your life. Christianity is about accepting the Lordship of Jesus and not just about accepting a saviour from sin. His Lordship should affect every area of our lives: our relationships, finances, habits, and so on.

As Christians, He is our Lord, and we are His servants. As servants, we do not own ourselves. Did you notice that Jesus is also called the "Captain of our salvation"? (Hebrews 2:10). He is not just our Saviour; He is the Captain of our salvation. And you know what? Those enlisted in the army with a captain over them take instructions from their captain. One says to one's captain, "Yes sir."

It is in light of this understanding that James warned us not to become boastful with our plans and live lives independent of God. While James wasn't against planning, he was warning against the spirit of independence from God.

James 4:13–16
^{13} Come now, you who say, "Today or tomorrow we will go to such and such a city, spend a year there, buy and sell, and make a profit";
^{14} Whereas you do not know what will happen tomorrow. For what is your life? It is even a vapour that appears for a little time and then vanishes away.
^{15} Instead you ought to say, "IF THE LORD WILLS, we shall live and do this or that."
^{16} But now you boast in your arrogance. All such boasting is evil.

Our attitude should be "if the Lord wills", because He is our Lord. Those who do not put God into consideration in decision-making will end up disappointed.

Servants begin by finding out their master's will and planning effectively.

God is our Master, and we are His servants.

I believe the best way for us to live and make the most important choices in life is to begin by asking the question, "What is the will of God in this situation?"

I once got a message from a member seeking my opinion about a forwarded text he received, concerning a single Christian sister who decided to do artificial insemination because she was getting old and had no suitors. Not wanting to go through her reproductive age without a child, she decided to do the insemination. Now the question is, "Did she sin, since she did not commit fornication with any man? And should she be disciplined by the church?"

My response was: The problem with sin is not about what one wants or desires but what God says. If we all follow our desires alone, then the logic will be that the man who stole is not a thief but that he is broke and without a job. Then what Achan did in the Old Testament and Ananias and Sapphira in the New Testament would be justified—but they paid for it.

There are two questions we need to ask ourselves in this case:
What is God's will in this matter? Should a child be born without a father figure? The answer is no. In God's agenda, children should be brought into the world in the context of marriage. The very first child born, Cain, was born to a couple, Adam and Eve. God's eternal plan has always been that children be raised in families! In Psalm 127:3–7 we are told, "Behold, children *are* a heritage from the LORD, the fruit of the womb *is* a reward. Like arrows in the hand of a warrior, so *are* the children of one's youth. **Happy is the man** who has his quiver full of them; they shall not be ashamed, But shall speak with their enemies in the gate." It is the man, not the woman, that is described as happy in these verses. The significance here is that children should be brought into the world in a home. Was she married in this case? No. Her desire to have a child cannot invalidate God's word.

Will God be glorified by this act? Can she stand in the congregation of the saints to give testimony to God for this act? The answer is an obvious no. What she did is no different from what Abram did when he entered Hagar, because he, too, had waited

(Genesis 16). It is not different from what Saul did, because he had waited for Samuel, and when he didn't see Samuel, he chose to offer the sacrifice (1 Samuel 13:11–15). We don't choose God's timing for Him. We wait until He is ready to bless us.

1 Samuel 13:11–15

¹¹ And Samuel said, "What have you done?" Saul said, "When I saw that the people were scattered from me, and *that* you did not come within the days appointed, and *that* the Philistines gathered together at Michmash,

¹² Then I said, 'The Philistines will now come down on me at Gilgal, and I have not made supplication to the LORD.' *Therefore, I felt compelled, and offered a burnt offering.*"

¹³ And Samuel said to Saul, "YOU HAVE DONE FOOLISHLY. You have not kept the commandment of the LORD your God, which He commanded you. For now the LORD would have established your kingdom over Israel forever.

¹⁴ But now your kingdom shall not continue. The LORD has sought for Himself a man after His own heart, and the LORD has commanded him *to be* commander over His people, because you have not kept what the LORD commanded you."

Just as Samuel told Saul, "You have done foolishly," I say to the sister, "It is a sin."

What is the lesson here? The moral filter through which we judge behaviours is not how we feel but what God's Word says.

If we, as Christians, will live out our lives in the consciousness of the will of God or the Word of God, we will experience a radical transformation in our lives.

There is no greater fulfilment in life than living one's life to the glory of God, to be like David, who served God's purpose for his generation, or like Paul, who confidently said, "I have finished my course" (Acts 13:36, 2 Timothy 4:7).

4.4

Complete Obedience Required

Our Master requires complete, not partial, obedience. One man who learned the hard way is Saul, the first king of Israel. In the fifteenth chapter of the first book of Samuel, he was given an explicit instruction—annihilate the Amalekites, both man and beast: leave nothing alive and take nothing back (1 Samuel 15:3).

The instruction was clear and straightforward, but Saul did not fully obey it, and Samuel informed him of this in the twenty-second and twenty-third verses:

1 Samuel 15:22–23
[22] Has the LORD as great delight in burnt offerings and sacrifices, as in obeying the voice of the LORD? *Behold, to obey is better than sacrifice, and to heed than the fat of rams.*
[23] For rebellion is as the sin of witchcraft, and stubbornness is as iniquity and idolatry. *Because you have rejected the word of the LORD, He also has rejected you from being king.*

God is our Master. He requires full obedience. Because Saul failed to comply, he was rejected as king.

Why did Saul fail? In the twentieth and twenty-first verses, we see the reason.

1 Samuel 15:20–21

²⁰ And Saul said to Samuel, "*But I have obeyed the voice of the* LORD, and gone on the mission on which the LORD sent me, and brought back Agag king of Amalek; I have utterly destroyed the Amalekites.

²¹ *But the people took of the plunder,* sheep and oxen, the best of the things which should have been utterly destroyed, to sacrifice to the LORD your God in Gilgal."

Saul said, "I did my part, but the people took of the plunder."

Our obedience should be to the Supreme Master of the Universe, and we shouldn't care what people think or how they feel about us. Perhaps Saul wanted to please the people and strengthen his position with them, but he ended up losing his kingship.

Once we know the divine instruction, no other opinion should sway us. Pleasing people at the expense of God is a recipe for disaster. Our attitudes should be as strong as those of Peter and John, who stood before the council and in the face of punishment, imprisonment and even death, said, "*We ought to obey God rather than men*" (Acts 5:29).

We should fear God to such an extent that we are willing to go to prison like Joseph rather than compromise with sin. We should fear God such that we are willing to be thrown into the burning furnace like Daniel's three friends rather than bow to Nebuchadnezzar's image of sin.

God is our Lord. In the Hebrew language, the title is "Adonai". And as our Lord, He requires our complete obedience. That's why Jesus asked us to pray, "Your will be done!"

Pray this with me: "Our Father, let Your will become the filter through which every decision in my life will be made. Help me to live my life in line with Your will, in Jesus' name."

5

Provider

Reference in the Lord's Prayer: **"Give us this day our daily bread."**

When Jesus asked them to pray, "Give us this day our daily bread", He revealed another hidden title of God, our Father: He is our Provider!

A critical role of being a father is meeting the needs of your family. I have two young kids who do not know the state of the economy of Nigeria or the meaning of the exchange rate. It is my responsibility to provide for them, irrespective of the economic situation. And in a challenging economy, I double my efforts to ensure that I give them the best quality of life I believe they deserve.

Do you think that I would be more interested in providing for the needs of my children than God, our heavenly Father, is for His children? Do you think you will be more responsible for your family than God is for His family?

Jesus used this concept to compare earthly fathers with our heavenly Father.

Matthew 7:9–11
⁹ Or what man is there among you who, if his son asks for bread, will give him a stone?
¹⁰ Or if he asks for a fish, will he give him a serpent?

¹¹ If you then, being evil, know how to give good gifts to your children, *how much more will your Father who is in heaven give good things to those who ask him*!

"How much more will your Father give good things to those who ask Him!" What a powerful thought. The best of men, with all their good deeds and philanthropic acts, pale into insignificance when compared with God, our Father.

When a child begins to worry about her father's ability to provide for her and meet her needs, then something is fundamentally wrong! Either she doesn't know her father's worth or doesn't trust him to honour his promises. In like manner, when the children of God begin to worry about God's ability to meet their needs, then something is fundamentally wrong too. It means we either do not know who our Father is or don't trust Him to honour His promises.

Matthew 6:25
²⁵ "THEREFORE I SAY TO YOU, DO NOT WORRY ABOUT YOUR LIFE, what you will eat or what you will drink; nor about your body, what you will put on. Is not life more than food and the body more than clothing?

This verse encourages and indicts us at the same time. It encourages us because it informs us about our Father's heart towards our every need, such as what we shall eat, drink, and wear. It indicts us because we do not genuinely believe in our Father's ability to meet our needs.

Matthew 6:26–30
²⁶ Look at the birds of the air, for they neither sow nor reap nor gather into barns; yet your heavenly Father feeds them. Are you not of more value than they?
²⁷ Which of you by worrying can add one cubit to his stature?
²⁸ So why do you worry about clothing? Consider the lilies of the field, how they grow: they neither toil nor spin;

²⁹ And yet I say to you that even Solomon in all his glory was not arrayed like one of these.

³⁰ Now if God so clothes the grass of the field, which today is, and tomorrow is thrown into the oven, will He not much more clothe you, O you of little faith?

If our heavenly Father cares enough about the birds of the air to feed them and the grass of the field to clothe them, how much more us His Children?

Worry is simply unbelief. It reveals that we do not trust God's ability to provide for us. I do not think that the children of Bill Gates or Jeff Bezos will ever worry about their school fees or their futures.

We worry because we do not know the worth and heart of our Father. All the wealth of the richest men and women in the world is less than one drop of water in the ocean of our Father's wealth, for the earth is the Lord's, and the fullness thereof (Psalm 24:1). The silver and gold belong to Him (Haggai 2:8); every beast of the forest is His, even the cattle upon a thousand hills (Psalm 50:10).

Our Father (the owner of the world's resources, the One, who is richer than all the richest men and women put together) is saying to you, "Do not worry about your life."

If we honestly believe in our Father's ability to meet our needs, we will live worry-free lives. God has made provision to adequately cater to our every need. And the best part of it is that the provision was made before the world began. Put another way, God provides for us before the need arises. He knows what we need and makes provision before we ask. It was God who saw that Adam needed a helper and provided Eve for him before Adam knew he needed a helper. That's the heart of our Father. He provides abundantly for us and in advance of our needs.

For every challenge facing you, God, your Father and Provider, has already made abundant provision available for you. For more on this, read my book *A YES GOD: God's Heart Concerning Your Needs*.

5.2

Jehovah-Jireh

Provision is a covenant promise that God had with the Israelites and that was revealed through the covenant name "Jehovah-Jireh".

Biblical scholars tell us that to understand a concept, we need to apply the principle of first mention, going back to the first place where the concept was mentioned and seeing the context in which it was used.

The first account of Jehovah-Jireh is seen in God's dealings with Abraham.

Genesis 22:14
[14] And Abraham called the name of the place, **The-Lord-Will-Provide**; as it is said to this day, "In the Mount of the Lord it shall be provided."

"The-Lord-Will-Provide" is the English translation of "Jehovah-Jireh".

As a background to the story in Genesis 22, God tested Abraham by asking him to sacrifice Isaac, his son, on one of the mountains He will show him. Abraham obeyed and embarked on the journey with Isaac.

Genesis 22:7–14

⁷ But Isaac spoke to Abraham his father and said, "My father!" And he said, "Here I am, my son." "Look, the fire and the wood, but where is the lamb for a burnt offering?"

⁸ And Abraham said, "MY SON, GOD WILL PROVIDE FOR HIMSELF THE LAMB FOR A BURNT OFFERING." So the two of them went together.

⁹ Then they came to the place of which God had told him. And Abraham built an altar there and placed the wood in order; and he bound Isaac his son and laid him on the altar, upon the wood.

¹⁰ And Abraham stretched out his hand and took the knife to slay his son.

¹¹ But the Angel of the LORD called to him from heaven and said, "Abraham, Abraham!" So he said, "Here I am."

¹² And He said, "Do not lay your hand on the lad, or do anything to him; for now I know that you fear God, since you have not withheld your son, your only son, from Me."

¹³ Then Abraham lifted his eyes and looked, AND THERE BEHIND HIM WAS A RAM CAUGHT IN A THICKET BY ITS HORNS. So Abraham went and took the ram, and offered it up for a burnt offering instead of his son.

¹⁴ And Abraham called the name of the place, The-LORD-Will-Provide; as it is said to this day, "In the Mount of the LORD it shall be provided."

The question I would like to address here is this: When was the ram provided—when Abraham stretched forth his hand to slay Isaac or before he got to the mountain?

I believe the ram was there waiting for Abraham's act of obedience. It was his faith and obedience that made him see the ram.

What do I mean? God did not intend for Abraham to kill Isaac; it was a test. Therefore, if God never intended for Abraham to kill Isaac, God must have provided for a substitute—the ram—long before Abraham got to the mountain. The ram was there waiting for Abraham's act of obedience before he could see it.

There are six essential lessons of Jehovah-Jireh in this passage worth considering:

- **God provides for every assignment He commissions us to carry out.** He will not instruct us to do something and then abandon us to provide for ourselves. Abraham knew this when he said to Isaac, "My son, God will provide for Himself the lamb for a burnt offering." God always provides for Himself. Minister of God, you don't need to put yourself or your people under a financial burden to give. If God asks you to do anything, He will provide for Himself. It is not your work but His. It is not your church but His, for He said, "I will build my Church" (Matthew 16:18). He is more than capable of financing His work.

    I am pained when I see believers in shopping malls and fuel stations begging strangers for money for a church-building project with a church project card. What a shame! It is an insult to the God we serve to beg strangers for His work. The early apostles refused to take money from the Gentiles for the work of God (3 John 7). Let us not bring God's name into disrepute. And let us stop putting God's people under a yoke of bondage to give. Our God is not poor. He will provide for Himself the lamb for the offering.

- **God provides ahead of our needs.** Before we get to the mountain, He has already made the provision available. For example, He provided for the children of Israel in Egypt. He knew they would need to build a tabernacle in the wilderness, so He provided for them long before the need arose (Exodus 12:35-36). And it was more than enough for the work; Moses had to restrain the people from giving (Exodus 36:5–6).

    As another example, Jesus is called "the lamb of God slain from the foundation of the world" (Revelation 13:8). That is, before man sinned, God had already made the provision for man's redemption. Amazing. No need takes God by surprise. You know why? He has made abundant supply available for all of humanity's needs from the foundation of the world (Hebrews 4:3).

- **God's provision requires faith and obedience.** Faith is the knowledge that "God will provide for Himself the lamb for the burnt offering." Obedience is acting based on faith: "and Abraham stretched out his hand and took the knife to slay his son." It takes faith (trusting in God's ability to provide) and obedience (taking steps even without seeing the physical manifestation of the provision) for us to see the provision.

- **The fact that we cannot see the provision doesn't mean that God has not provided.** The ram was kept behind Abraham. "Then Abraham lifted his eyes and looked, and *there behind him was a ram caught* in a thicket by its horns." Real faith is not looking forward but looking back to Calvary, God's eternal provision, and drawing from it to meet our needs.

- **God provides when we are in the right place.** "In the Mount of the Lord it shall be provided." Many times, we run helter-skelter looking for answers instead of seeking God's face. Provision happens only in the Mount of the Lord, in the presence of Jehovah.

- **God has not stopped providing.** He did not provide for Abraham and stopped providing afterwards. It wasn't a once-in-a-lifetime provision. As it is said to this day, "In the Mount of the Lord it shall be provided." To this day, God has not stopped providing. He is still meeting people's needs all over the world, because He is our Jehovah-Jireh.

God has not stopped being our Jehovah-Jireh. He still supplies all our needs according to His riches in glory in Christ Jesus (Philippians 4:19).

The implication of, "Give us *this day* our daily bread", is that we are supposed to receive the bread daily to *this day*. Our Father is our Jehovah-Jireh, still providing for our needs to this day.

Today is your day of provision. In this prayer, we see someone who knows the heart of the Father. There is a daily provision for you from the storehouse of heaven. "Blessed be the Lord, *who daily loads us with benefits.* The God of our salvation! Selah" (Psalm 68:19).

How often do we receive our benefits? Daily!

In what measure? Loads of benefits.

The picture I see in my spirit is an overflow of blessing. When you load someone with something, you are giving that person more than he or she needs. We call it an extra portion or double dose just like Joseph gave Benjamin five times more than his brothers (Genesis 43:34). God daily loads us with benefits. He gives us in "good measure, pressed down, shaken together, and running over," "much more than we can ever ask or think" (Luke 6:38, Ephesians 3:20).

There is a daily load of benefits from the throne room of grace. Our God, the God of our salvation, did not save us and just leave us alone to cater for ourselves. He daily loads us with benefits.

Have you received yours today?

5.3

Can God Prepare a Table in the Wilderness?

Our problems as they relate to receiving from God are twofold: faith and obedience. Faith believes that everything God says He is, He is, and that everything He says He will do, He will do; obedience acts on that knowledge.

The children of Israel got to the point where they lost the idea of the greatness of God and tempted Him in the wilderness:

Psalm 78:17–20
[17] But they sinned even more against Him by rebelling against the Most High in the wilderness.
[18] And they tested God in their heart by asking for the food of their fancy.
[19] Yes, they spoke against God: THEY SAID, "CAN GOD PREPARE A TABLE IN THE WILDERNESS?
[20] Behold, He struck the rock, so that the waters gushed out, and the streams overflowed. Can He give bread also? Can He provide meat for His people?"

The question the children of Israel asked in the wilderness is the same question we ask today: Can God bless me where I am?

The Israelites got to the point where they looked at the wilderness, their current experience, and concluded that God couldn't meet their needs in the wilderness. They knew that God could bring forth water from a rock (an impossible situation), but they doubted His ability to provide bread for them. And when they did so, they provoked God to anger.

Psalm 78:40–42
⁴⁰ How often they ***provoked Him*** in the wilderness, and grieved Him in the desert!

⁴¹ Yes, again and again they tempted God, and ***limited the Holy One of Israel***.

⁴² ***They did not remember His power***: the day when he redeemed them from the enemy.

They limited the limitless One, for Whom nothing is impossible. You see that it wasn't the wilderness that limited God; it was their unbelief.

And why did they limit Him? They did so because "they did not remember His power: the day when He redeemed them from the enemy."

Their biggest problem was that they forgot about their redemption. In this verse, we see that had they remembered the day God redeemed them from the enemy in Egypt, they would have known that providing meat for them in the wilderness was nothing compared to what God had already done for them. That is, the miracle of redemption is far greater than the blessing of provision.

Today I think this is the biggest problem of the Church when it comes to receiving from God. We have forgotten what God did for us when He redeemed us from the power of the enemy. We have forgotten that our redemption is the biggest act of deliverance that God will ever do for us, and if He has done that for us, nothing else is too hard for Him to do. Let me put it this way: redemption is far more difficult than provision, and if God has already secured our redemption, then meeting our needs is far too easy for Him to do. Is it possible that someone who can move mountains cannot pick up a stone?

Romans 8:32
³² He who did not spare His own Son, but delivered Him up for us all, *how shall He not with Him also freely give us all things?*

If God did not spare His own Son but delivered Him up for us all (for our redemption), how shall He not with Him also *freely* give us all things (provision)?

As I was writing this, God opened my eyes to see that there is only one price to pay—the price for our redemption. And that price was paid when He gave up Jesus for us; everything else is *freely given!*

Until we get this revelation into your spirit, you will still struggle with receiving your provision from God.

God is limited not by our economic situation but by our unbelief. Unbelief manifests in one of two ways: stubbornness or ignorance. In stubbornness, the person knows the truth but refuses to believe it; in ignorance, the person believes otherwise because he doesn't know the truth.

I believe most believers suffer from the sin of unbelief through ignorance. This kind of unbelief can be cured through revelation. The more of God we know, the more easily we can trust Him.

Don't compartmentalize God. God, who can save, can also provide. God, who can deliver from sin, can also deliver from poverty.

Two questions we must settle about this great God are the following:

Can God provide? It's a question of ability.

Will God provide? It's a question of willingness.

God can and is ever willing to provide for us. He "is able to do exceedingly abundantly above all that we ask or think, according to the power that works in us" (Ephesians 3:20).

David knew God's ability and willingness to provide when he said, "You prepare a table before me in the presence of my enemies" (Psalm 23:5).

God is our Master Chef. As our Lord, we are His servants, and we wait on Him. As our Provider, God reverses the equation and serves us. He waits on us.

Enjoy the meal. God has already prepared a table for you. I think the problem with many Christians is that rather than enjoying what God has provided, they are busy looking at their wilderness or their enemies.

Enjoy your meal. God has provided a table for you!

5.4

Is God against Prosperity?

Many have told lies against God. They have said:
God does not want you to prosper!
God wants you to be poor!
Prosperity is of the devil!

It is a lie of the devil that poverty is a mark of spirituality and that we should barely survive as we make it through life. We do not have any problem with unbelievers being successful and wealthy, but many have a problem with believers being successful and wealthy. Why is that?

God is not against your prosperity; He provided abundantly for Adam in the garden. The garden of Eden was a garden of abundance (Genesis 1:28–30).

God wants you to have a prosperous journey (Joshua 1:8). He isn't against your prosperity; He is against covetousness. A prosperous person has enough to meet his needs and help others in need; a covetous or greedy person is never satisfied with what he has, no matter the amount. And because he is never satisfied, he is stingy even when he has a lot.

I want to leave you with some Scriptures to prove to you that God is not against your prosperity:

Genesis 24:1

¹ Now Abraham was old, well advanced in age; **and the LORD had blessed Abraham in all things.**

Job 36:11

¹¹ If they obey and serve Him, **they shall spend their days in prosperity**, and their years in pleasures.

Psalm 35:27

²⁷ Let them shout for joy and be glad, who favour my righteous cause; and let them say continually, "Let the LORD be magnified, **who has pleasure in the prosperity of His servant.**"

3 John 2

² Beloved, I pray that **you may prosper in all things** and be in health, just as your soul prospers.

These verses are clear about God's will concerning your life. Prosperity is part of God's promise for your life. Believe it and trust Him to meet all your needs. He is your Shepherd, and you shall not want (Psalm 23:1).

2 Corinthians 9:8

⁸ And God is able to make all grace abound towards you, that you, always having all sufficiency in all things, *may have an abundance for every good work.*

Why does God want you to be prosperous? The goal of prosperity is to help you fulfil your purpose and be a blessing to others in His name. It is to make you a channel of blessing to others—the conduit of God's love in a tangible form to a dying world.

You are not rich because of what you have but because of the people you have been a blessing to. The Lord told Abram, "I will bless you . . . and you shall be a blessing" (Genesis 12:2).

Don't become like the rich fool. He was blessed, but he forgot the purpose of the blessing (Luke 12:15–21). Money is not an end in itself; it is a means to an end. And God is not against you having loads of it as long as you use it to His glory by being a blessing to others.

2 Corinthians 9:12–13

[12] For the administration of this service not only SUPPLIES THE NEEDS OF THE SAINTS, but also is abounding through many thanksgivings to God,

[13] While, through the proof of this ministry, THEY GLORIFY GOD for the obedience of your confession to the gospel of Christ, and FOR YOUR LIBERAL SHARING WITH THEM AND ALL MEN. . . .

6

Healer

Reference in the Lord's Prayer: **"Give us this day our daily bread."**

Is there a direct reference to healing in the Lord's prayer? No. But any student of the Bible would know that healing must be a part of the package of our faith in Christ Jesus and in the Lord's Prayer.

Our reference to healing is in Matthew 15:21–28. When Jesus came into the region of Tyre and Sidon, a Canaanite woman pleaded with Him to heal her severely demon-oppressed daughter.

Matthew 15:26
²⁶ But He answered and said, "IT IS NOT GOOD TO TAKE THE CHILDREN'S BREAD and throw *it* to the little dogs."

Jesus called healing in this account "the children's bread". And if He asked us to pray, "Give us this day our daily bread," then healing must be an integral part of our daily bread.

Continuing the passage, the woman whose daughter was called a dog, as it were, was not angry at the statement.

Matthew 15:27–28
²⁷ And she said, "Yes, Lord, yet even the little dogs eat the crumbs which fall from their masters' table."

²⁸ Then Jesus answered and said to her, "O woman, great *is* your faith! Let it be to you as you desire." And her daughter was healed from that very hour.

The woman's daughter was healed with the crumbs. She had so much faith in the bread that she believed the crumbs would be enough to heal her daughter. How amazing. If the woman's daughter was healed with crumbs, how much more will we, the children of the kingdom that the bread was made for, be healed?

Healing is your birthright. Did you notice that Jesus spent more time casting out demons and healing the sick than in any other aspects of His ministry?

Today we preach an intellectual and philosophical Jesus, the Jesus of principles, appealing to the intellect of men. This is not bad, because Jesus is the greatest teacher who ever walked the earth. But if we teach only an intellectual Jesus, we deprive the world of the blessing of the fullness of the gospel in Christ Jesus.

Some also preach a social crusader and social justice reformer Jesus with a focus on politics and social reform. While this is good, Jesus is much more than a political reformer.

Any message about Jesus that doesn't include healing deprives the world of the full package of redemption. Healing was so integral to His commission that if we were to remove it, we would have removed an integral part of His message and commission.

Matthew 4:23–24
²³ And Jesus went about all Galilee, teaching in their synagogues, preaching the gospel of the kingdom, and *healing all kinds of sickness* and *all kinds of disease* among the people.

²⁴ Then His fame went throughout all Syria, and they brought to Him all sick people who were afflicted with various diseases and torments, and

those who were demon-possessed, epileptics, and paralytics; and He healed them.

We see another confirmation in Matthew 14:34–36.

Matthew 14:34–36
³⁴ When they had crossed over, they came to the land of Gennesaret.
³⁵ And when the men of that place recognized Him, they sent out into all that surrounding region, brought to Him all who were sick,
³⁶ And begged Him that they might only touch the hem of His garment. And as many as touched it were made perfectly well.

The name "Jesus" was synonymous with healing then. Even His commission in Acts 10:38 has healing as an integral part of His assignment.

Acts 10:38
How God anointed Jesus of Nazareth with the Holy Spirit and with power, who went about doing good and **healing all who were oppressed by the devil**, for God was with Him.

6.2

Does God Still Heal Today?

The challenge for many is not whether Jesus healed then but whether He will heal today. That is, does God still heal today?

The answer is simple. If healing is not for today, then salvation is also not for today, because the promise of salvation and healing go together.

Isaiah 53 has been described as a messianic chapter because it clearly illustrates the sufferings and provisions of the coming Messiah. In that chapter, we see that forgiveness of sins and healing for the body go together.

Isaiah 53:4–6
⁴ Surely He has borne our griefs and carried our sorrows; yet we esteemed Him stricken, smitten by God, and afflicted.
⁵ But He was wounded for our transgressions, He was bruised for our iniquities; the chastisement for our peace was upon Him, and BY HIS STRIPES WE ARE HEALED.
⁶ All we like sheep have gone astray; we have turned, every one, to his own way; and the Lord has laid on Him the iniquity of us all.

The same chapter that tells us that "He was wounded for our transgressions" and "bruised for our iniquities" also tells us that "by His stripes we are healed."

If healing is not for today, then salvation is also not for today.

If healing is not for today, then we cannot lay claim to having peace with God, because the verse that reads "the chastisement for our peace was upon Him" also reads "by His stripes we are healed."

Jesus came as our sin-bearer and sickness-healer. Peter confirmed this promise many centuries after Isaiah when he said, "Who Himself bore our sins in His own body on the tree, that we, having died to sins, might live for righteousness—**by whose stripes you were healed**" (1 Peter 2:24). This verse is a perfect summary of Isaiah's prophecy of the Messiah. He bore our sins, and by His stripes we were healed.

Because Jesus is the same yesterday, today, and forever (Hebrews 13:8), healing is for today. It is part of your redemptive rights and your provision in Christ Jesus. Receive it by faith.

6.3

How Many Will God Heal?

Now that we know that healing is still relevant today, the question remains: How many will God heal?

To answer this question, we need to see how many God healed during the time of Jesus.

Matthew 8:16
16 When evening had come, they brought to Him many who were demon-possessed. And He cast out the spirits with a word, and HEALED ALL WHO WERE SICK.

Matthew 12:15
15 And great multitudes followed Him, and HE HEALED THEM ALL.

Matthew 14:34–36
34 When they had crossed over, they came to the land of Gennesaret.
35 And when the men of that place recognized Him, they sent out into all that surrounding region, BROUGHT TO HIM ALL WHO WERE SICK,
36 And begged Him that they might only touch the hem of His garment. AND AS MANY AS TOUCHED IT WERE MADE PERFECTLY WELL.

Luke 6:19
19 And the whole multitude sought to touch Him, for power went out from Him and HEALED THEM ALL.

So how many will God heal today? If He healed all then, He will heal all now.

Healing is your birthright. Receive it with thanksgiving in Jesus' name.

When Jesus asked us to pray, "Give us this day our daily bread," it means you can be healed today. Don't postpone your healing. Sickness does not glorify God in any way. The glory of God is seen in your healing and deliverance.

God is our healer. The covenant name to the Israelites is "Jehovah-Rapha", as first revealed in Exodus 15:26: "If you diligently heed the voice of the Lord your God and do what is right in His sight, give ear to His commandments and keep all His statutes, I will put none of the diseases on you which I have brought on the Egyptians. FOR I AM THE LORD WHO HEALS YOU."

"I am the Lord who heals you" means God wants you well and whole, not sick. God will not use sickness to teach you a lesson. He wants to heal your body of every disease. God wants saved spirits, renewed minds, and whole bodies.

Exodus 23:25
So you shall serve the Lord your God, and He will bless your bread and your water. AND I WILL TAKE SICKNESS AWAY FROM THE MIDST OF YOU.

"I will take sickness away from the midst of you" means that none of us should be sick. This may sound difficult, but I choose to believe this promise.

7

Holy God

Reference in the Lord's Prayer: "**And forgive us our debts.**"

When Jesus asked His disciples to pray, "And forgive us our debts", He revealed another hidden title of God: The Holy God.

If God were not a holy God, there wouldn't have been the need to ask for the forgiveness of our debts, as there would be no standard by which to judge our actions.

If God were not a holy God, then redemption would not have been necessary in the first place.

God is a holy God. His holiness is the standard by which our actions are judged. "Talk no more so very proudly; let no arrogance come from your mouth, for the Lord is the God of knowledge; *and by Him actions are weighed*" (1 Samuel 2:3).

God is the standard by which all our actions are weighed. And when our actions fall short of His standard, we call them sins, but they are also debts that we owe God—debts we must pay.

The debate about what our debts represent can be put to rest by reading Matthew 18:21–35, although it is too long to quote here.

The passage begins with a question about sin: Then Peter came to Him and said, "Lord, **how often shall my brother sin against me**, and I forgive him? Up to seven times?" [21].

Jesus replied by giving a parable about debt and forgiveness.

Matthew 18:22–27
[22] Jesus said to him, "I do not say to you, up to seven times, but up to seventy times seven.
[23] Therefore the kingdom of heaven is like a certain king who wanted to settle accounts with his servants.
[24] And when he had begun to settle accounts, one was brought to him who owed him ten thousand talents.
[25] But as he was not able to pay, his master commanded that he be sold, with his wife and children and all that he had, and that payment be made.
[26] The servant therefore fell down before him, saying, 'Master, have patience with me, and I will pay you all.'
[27] Then the master of that servant was moved with compassion, released him, and **forgave him the debt**."

Jesus ended the parable by talking about trespasses and forgiveness.

Matthew 18:35
[35] So My heavenly Father also will do to you if each of you, from his heart, does not **forgive his brother his trespasses**.

The passage started with a question about sin but ended with a parable about debt, trespasses, and forgiveness. "Sin", "debt", and "trespasses" are used interchangeably in this passage, and I want to use them interchangeably too and not be bothered about the nuances.

When Jesus asked us to pray to God to forgive us our debts, He revealed God as the holy God, the God who will not condone sin. "You are of purer eyes than to behold evil, and cannot look on wickedness" (Habakkuk 1:13). God will not condone, support, or celebrate evil, because of His holy nature.

Psalm 5:4–6
⁴ FOR YOU ARE NOT A GOD WHO TAKES PLEASURE IN WICKEDNESS, nor shall evil dwell with You.
⁵ The boastful shall not stand in Your sight; YOU HATE ALL WORKERS OF INIQUITY.
⁶ You shall destroy those who speak falsehood; The Lord abhors the bloodthirsty and deceitful man.

The concept of the holiness of God is a theme that runs all through the Bible, the most famous passage being Isaiah 6:3:

Isaiah 6:3
³ And one cried to another and said: "HOLY, HOLY, HOLY is the Lord of hosts; The whole earth is full of His glory!"

God is holy—so holy that it was repeated thrice. No other attribute of God in the whole Bible is repeated three times in this manner.

What does the holiness of God mean?

There are two root meanings of the word "holy": (1) to be distinct or separate, and (2) to be morally pure—incapable of sinning. Combining both, our Father is so pure in thought, character, and actions that He is incapable of ever sinning and therefore stands alone, different, and distinct from all others.

It is God's holiness that sets Him apart from all other gods.

Exodus 15:11
¹¹ Who is like You, O Lord, among the gods?
WHO IS LIKE YOU, GLORIOUS IN HOLINESS,
Fearful in praises, doing wonders?

1 Samuel 2:2
² NO ONE IS HOLY LIKE THE LORD,
For there is none besides You,
Nor is there any rock like our God.

Isaiah 40:25
²⁵ "To whom, then, will you liken Me,
or TO WHOM SHALL I BE EQUAL?" SAYS THE HOLY ONE.

These three verses inform us that God is unlike any other in holiness. God is so holy that all others are wretched and vile before Him.

We serve a holy God. Under the Old Covenant, the high priest had a sign on the turban on his forehead with the inscription, "Holiness unto the Lord" (Exodus 28:36).

When Jesus asked us to pray, "And forgive us our debts", He was reminding us of this attribute of God—He is a holy God!

7.2

Everything about God Is Holy

God is so holy that everything about Him—His person, attributes, people, and service—is holy. Isaiah repeatedly called Him "The Holy One of Israel."

> Exodus 3:5: The ground where God is, is holy.
> Exodus 12:16: The convocation to the Lord is holy.
> Exodus 15;13: His habitation is holy.
> Exodus 16:23: The Sabbath is holy.
> Leviticus 2:3: His offerings are holy.
> 2 Chronicles 35:3: The ark is holy.
> Nehemiah 11:1: Jerusalem is called the holy city.
> Psalm 11:4: His temple is holy.
> Psalm 20:6: Heaven is holy.
> Psalm 33:21: His name is holy.
> Psalm 55:11: His Spirit is holy.
> Psalm 89:20: His oil is holy.
> Psalm 105:42: His promise is holy.
> Psalm 145:17: All His works are holy.
> 2 Peter 2:21: His commandment is holy.
> 2 Timothy 3:15: The Scriptures are holy.

As God's people, we are to
be holy people unto the Lord (Leviticus 20:26),
be holy as God is holy (1 Peter 1:16),
be holy in our conversation and conduct (1 Peter 1:15, 2 Peter 3:11),
greet one another with a holy kiss (2 Corinthians 13:12), and
lift up holy hands (1 Timothy 2:8).

8

Merciful God

Reference in the Lord's Prayer: **"And forgive us our debts."**

When Jesus asked His disciples to pray, "And forgive us our debts", He revealed another hidden title of God: The Merciful God!

If God were only a holy God and nothing else, then, like Isaiah, we will all stand condemned before Him. When Isaiah saw the holiness of God in Isaiah 6, he said of himself, "*Woe is me, for I am undone*! Because I am a man of unclean lips, and I dwell in the midst of a people of unclean lips, for My eyes have seen the King, The LORD of Hosts" (Isaiah 6:5).

God's holiness revealed Isaiah's wretchedness, "I am undone."

Before this encounter, Isaiah had been heaping and prophesying woe unto the people (Isaiah 5:8, 11, 18, 21–23). He stood dignified in self-righteousness. But when he saw God in His holiness, he knew that he was not different from the people he had been prophesying woe unto, "Because I am a man of unclean lips, and I dwell in the midst of a people of unclean lips." He, too, did not meet God's holy standard.

God's holiness makes our righteousness appear like filthy rags before Him (Isaiah 64:6). Our self-righteousness is like the fig leaves that Adam and Eve used to cover their nakedness—inadequate to allow us to stand before a holy God.

Another person who encountered God's holiness and changed his perspective about God was Job. He maintained his innocence before his friends and felt he could argue his righteousness before God. But when he saw God in His holiness, he answered the Lord: "Behold, I am vile; what shall I answer You? I lay my hand over my mouth. Once I have spoken, but I will not answer; yes, twice, but I will proceed no further" (Job 40:4–5).

God's holiness revealed Job's wretchedness: "*Behold, I am vile.*"

God's holiness silenced every argument and self-righteousness that Job had before that moment: "*I lay my hand over my mouth.*"

Before God's holiness, we become speechless and cannot utter a word: "*What shall I answer You?*"

But thank God that God is not just a holy God; He is also a merciful God. While the holy God will not overlook sin, the merciful God makes provisions for our sins to be forgiven.

Continuing with Isaiah's encounter with the holiness of God in Isaiah 6, we see what God did.

Isaiah 6:6–7
⁶ Then one of the seraphim flew to me, having in his hand a live coal which he had taken with the tongs from the altar.
⁷ And he touched my mouth with it, and said: "Behold, this has touched your lips; *your iniquity is taken away, and your sin purged.*"

Isn't it comforting to know that God is a merciful God? The angel touched his mouth and said, "Your iniquity is taken away, and your sin purged."

To purge is to remove completely, to separate something from another. So when God forgives, He completely removes our sin, such that we stand before Him as if we had never sinned. Thank you, Lord!

Isaiah 43:25

25 "I, even I, am He who blots out your transgressions for My own sake; AND I WILL NOT REMEMBER YOUR SINS."

8.2

Completely Forgiven

When God forgives, He completely erases the event from our records in heaven and from His memory.

The passage in Matthew 18:22–35 quoted earlier is relevant here. After Peter asked about how many times he should forgive his brother, Jesus gave a parable of forgiveness using the servant who couldn't pay his debt, to teach Peter the real meaning of forgiveness.

Matthew 18:25–27
[25] But as he was not able to pay, his master commanded that he be sold, with his wife and children and all that he had, and that payment be made.
[26] The servant therefore fell down before him, saying, "Master, have patience with me, and I will pay you all."
[27] Then the master of that servant *was moved with compassion, released him, and forgave him the debt.*

I want you to pay particular attention to the twenty-seventh verse. Three keywords in the verse are "compassion", "release", and "forgiveness".

From this verse, we see that forgiveness is the end result of compassion and release. This can alternatively be illustrated as follows:

Forgiveness = Compassion + Release

True forgiveness is showing compassion to someone and releasing that individual from every obligation attached to his debt by cancelling that debt. This means discharging the person and setting him free from every indebtedness. It means resetting the person's account to zero by wiping out all his obligations. And this must be done with compassion, out of love, and not through coercion or grudgingness.

Grudgingness = Release – Compassion
Sympathy = Compassion – Release

We are all like the servant in the parable. We cannot truly settle our accounts with our King. The Bible says that if God were to mark iniquities and record them, no one could stand before Him (Psalm 130:3), so in His mercy, He has made forgiveness possible.

I want you to consider the meaning of forgiveness again. To forgive someone who owes you a lot of money is to bear the loss of the amount while the person is released completely free. Now you understand why Jesus had to die for our forgiveness. God had to bear the loss in Christ Jesus so that we can walk free. Our debts were transferred to the person of Jesus, and our records were expunged once and for all.

I will now relate to you three Scriptures that gladden my heart when I think about God's forgiveness.

Psalm 103:8, 10–12

[8] The LORD is merciful and gracious,
Slow to anger, and abounding in mercy.
[10] He has not dealt with us according to our sins,
Nor punished us according to our iniquities.
11 For as the heavens are high above the earth,
So great is His mercy toward those who fear Him;
[12] As far as the east is from the west, so far has He removed our transgressions from us.

Here we see certain qualities about God's mercy and how God deals with our sins.

His nature: "The Lord is merciful and gracious, slow to anger, and abounding in mercy."

His attitude towards our sins: "He does not deal with us according to our sins or punish us according to our iniquities." If God were to deal with us according to our sins or punish us according to our iniquities, we would all be destroyed. It is a lie from the pit of hell that God is punishing you for your sins; your sins were punished in Christ Jesus. God doesn't deal with us according to our sins.

The extent of His mercy: His mercy is as great as "the heavens are higher than the earth". Just as we cannot measure the distance between the heavens and the earth, we cannot completely fathom the heights and depths of God's mercy towards us.

The removal of our sins: He removes our transgressions from us "as the east is far from the west". Why did the Psalmist use the east and the west and not the north and the south? We know from elementary geography that the earth has four cardinal poles—north, south, east, and west. What we were not told is that while the north and south poles lie on a straight line and one can travel from the north pole to the south pole and vice versa, the east and west poles do not meet. One cannot travel from the east pole and arrive at the west pole; it is an impossibility. So God's removal of our sins as far as the east is from the west means our sins have been completely separated from us and can never again be used against us before God, just as the east can never meet the west. "As far as the east is from the west …" That's infinity; so also is our forgiveness.

Micah 7:19
[19] He will again have compassion on us, **and will subdue our iniquities**.

You will **cast all our sins into the depths of the sea**.

Did you notice that God "will subdue our iniquities"? It implies that our iniquities will be completely defeated and will not raise their ugly heads against us.

How will He subdue them? By casting them into the depths of the sea, where no one can ever find them.

When did He subdue them? On the cross.

Who subdued them for us? Jesus Christ.

My brother and sister in Christ, your iniquities have been subdued and swallowed by the blood of Jesus.

Hebrews 8:12
[12] For I will be merciful to their unrighteousness, and *their sins and their lawless deeds I will remember no more.*

When God forgives, He forgets; He deletes the record completely from His memory. And if God does not keep a record of our sins when He forgives us, why keep yours?

When Balak contracted with Balaam to curse the children of Israel, God gave us a glimpse of His forgiveness in Balaam's prophecy: "*He has not observed iniquity in Jacob*, nor has He seen wickedness in Israel. The Lord his God is with him, And the shout of a King is among them" (Numbers 23:21).

We know that the children of Israel were stubborn people, and their stubbornness cost Moses the promised land, yet God said to Balaam, "I have not observed iniquity in Jacob." God doesn't keep a record of our wrongdoings.

When Peter came to the Master and asked Him how many times he should forgive his brother, he missed the point. It is not about the number of times. If you are keeping a record of the number of times you have forgiven someone, you have not forgiven that person. Love, as we are informed, "keeps no record of wrongs" (1 Corinthians 13:5 NIV). Jesus used the parable of the king that completely discharged his debtor as an example of real forgiveness.

When God forgives, He shreds the record!

Colossians 2:14 NLT
[11] He CANCELLED the record of the charges against us and TOOK IT AWAY by nailing it to the cross.

The record of your charges has been cancelled. Celebrate your forgiveness.

8.3

Come Boldly to Obtain Forgiveness

When Jesus asked us to pray, "and forgive us our debts", He wasn't condoning sin, but He knew that we would make mistakes in our walk with God. And at such times when we fall, rather than running away as Adam did, we should approach our Father and ask for forgiveness.

Hebrews 4:15–16
¹⁵ For we do not have a High Priest who cannot sympathize with our weaknesses, but was in all points tempted as we are, yet without sin.
¹⁶ Let us therefore COME BOLDLY TO THE THRONE OF GRACE, THAT WE MAY OBTAIN MERCY and find grace to help in time of need.

The context of coming boldly to the throne of grace is our struggles with temptations. The writer of Hebrews said at such times when we fall into sin, we should "come boldly to the throne of grace" so that we can "obtain mercy and find grace to help in time of need."

The throne of grace has two provisions: mercy for the sins we just committed, and grace to help us overcome the temptation the next time.

Rather than condemn yourself for your sins and trespasses, come boldly to the throne of grace, because Jesus is not only your High Priest before the throne, He is also your Advocate before the Father (1 John 2:1).

One day, as I was meditating on the ministry of my Advocate, God gave me the words to this song:

> My Advocate with the Father
> Is Jesus, the Son of God,
> Who pleads my case with the Father
> That I might be justified.

You have an advocate before the Father. He is Jesus, the Son of God. Who is better to plead your case? He is standing in God's presence on your behalf (Hebrews 9:24). Don't run away. When you run away, it means you do not have faith in the ministry of your Advocate. Come boldly and obtain mercy and find grace to help in the time of need.

8.4

Apply the Blood

If God has completely forgiven us and erased our record, why do we still struggle with condemnation in our conscience? Because we do not know the power of God's forgiveness.

If we know that we are completely forgiven, then we know that the devil is powerless to accuse us before God. So what does he do? He accuses us in our conscience.

For those struggling with condemnation in their conscience, here is a verse of Scripture that will help you.

Hebrews 9:14
[14] How much more SHALL THE BLOOD OF CHRIST, who through the eternal Spirit offered Himself without spot to God, CLEANSE YOUR CONSCIENCE from dead works to serve the living God?

Apply the blood of Jesus to your conscience! The blood of Jesus not only deletes our records in heaven but also purges our consciences of the effect of sin.

The blood of Christ will cleanse your conscience from dead works: the works of personal atonement—attempts to appease God with our flesh to make up for our sins.

As you confess your forgiveness through the blood of Christ, the hold of condemnation of sin over your life will be broken.

You are forgiven. Don't allow the devil to tell you otherwise!

9

The Restorer of Broken Relationships

Reference in the Lord's Prayer: **"As we forgive our debtors."**

When Jesus asked His disciples to pray, "And forgive us our debts as we forgive our debtors", He revealed another hidden title of God: The Restorer of Broken Relationships.

Just as our sins weigh us down and make us want to run away from God's presence, when others offend us, they are also weighed down by guilt and want to run away from our presence. Since God is a merciful God, He expects us to be merciful to others and to forgive their debts just as He has forgiven ours. "Therefore be merciful, just as your Father also is merciful" (Luke 6:36).

Many people behave as if they are holier than God. In their defence of righteousness and standing for what is right, they have refused to show mercy to people or forgive them for their mistakes. They come down hard on others. Sometimes, even when others have asked them for mercy and forgiveness, they still cannot forgive. They ruminate on why the other person made the mistake in the first place. They believe everybody should be perfect "like them", even though they know they are not perfect. They have become, in attitude, no different from the Pharisees.

You cannot be holier than God. If the Holy God can forgive you, then who are you not to forgive others?

God expects us to forgive others in the same manner as He forgives us—to cast their sins into the depths of the sea and remember them no more.

9.2

The Cost of Failing to Forgive

Did you notice that the prayer for forgiveness from God has one condition? It is the only aspect of the Lord's prayer with a conditional requirement on our part.

"And forgive us our debts **as** we forgive our debtors."

To experience God's forgiveness, we need to forgive others. Put literally, Jesus said, "Do you want God to forgive your debts and trespasses? Then learn to forgive others."

If God is our Father, it means we are already saved, so the forgiveness here is not about the original Adamic sin but the besetting sins in our journey through life (Hebrews 12:1).

In our interactions with people, both believers and unbelievers, we will be hurt, wounded, and offended, but God still expects us to forgive nonetheless. It doesn't matter about the nature of the sins against us; just as we expect God to forgive us, we too must forgive others.

In the parable of forgiveness in Matthew 18:21–35, after the servant that owed his master ten thousand talents was forgiven, he went out and saw a fellow servant who owed him one hundred denarii.

What did he do?

Matthew 18:28–30

²⁸ But that servant went out and found one of his fellow servants who owed him a hundred denarii; and he laid hands on him and took him by the throat, saying, "Pay me what you owe!"

²⁹ So his fellow servant fell down at his feet and begged him, saying, "Have patience with me, and I will pay you all."

³⁰ *And he would not, but went and threw him into prison till he should pay the deb*t.

Wow. Such a wicked heart!

To appreciate the wickedness of this servant, we need to consider his debt to his master with the debt of his fellow servant to him.

Various scholars have calculated the exact amount in today's currency differently. Some equate ten thousand talents to millions of dollars, and others to billions of dollars, but one hundred denarii is quite small; some say it is less than $100 today. The absolute figure is not important. What is important is that his huge and almost impossible-to-pay debt was cancelled, yet he couldn't forgive someone of a very insignificant amount.

However, I believe a better way to look at this parable is to focus not so much on the monetary value but rather on how long it takes to repay each debt.

A denarius is a day's wage. So, one hundred denarii will be repaid in a hundred workdays. Since the average Jewish worker at the time of Jesus worked for three hundred days (excluding the Sabbath and Jewish holidays), this debt would be repaid in about four months.

However, one talent is the equivalent of six thousand denarii, or twenty years of work. Therefore, ten thousand talents would take *two hundred thousand years* to repay (others put it at one hundred fifty thousand years). Whether it is one hundred and fifty thousand or two hundred thousand years, think of how many lifetimes you would need to repay the debt.

Now you understand the enormity of his debt and the extent of the master's forgiveness and the wickedness of the servant when he failed to forgive his fellow servant who owed him a pittance.

The fellow servants who saw what he did reported the case to the master.

Matthew 18:32–34

³² Then his master, after he had called him, said to him, "You wicked servant! I forgave you all that debt because you begged me.
³³ ***Should you not also have had compassion on your fellow servant, just as I had pity on you?***"
³⁴ And his master was angry, and delivered him to the torturers until he should pay all that was due to him.

Jesus concluded the parable by saying, "So my heavenly Father also will do to you if each of you, from his heart, does not forgive his brother his trespasses" (Matthew 18:35).

The essence of this parable is that there is nothing someone owes us or has done against us that can be compared to what we owe God and have done against Him. And if God can forgive and completely discharge us from our sins, we ought also to forgive and completely discharge our brothers and sisters from their wrongdoings against us.

We can never repay what we owe God, so in His infinite mercy, He chose to forgive us completely. What does our fellow brother or sister owe us that we cannot forgive him or her?

If God does not hold our sins against us or count them against us, we ought also not hold the sins of our fellow brothers and sisters against them.

When we fail to forgive, we invalidate God's forgiveness over our lives. Notice that although the master forgave the servant in the parable—an act of mercy and grace—when he failed to forgive his fellow servant and demanded that his fellow servant repay his debt, he was living based on the law and the principle of justice. Therefore, the master invalidated his act of mercy and grace over him and applied the same principle of law and justice.

When we fail to forgive, we invalidate God's forgiveness over our lives because we are operating under the law and not under grace. And guess what? It will take eternity for us to repay our debts under the principle of law and justice, and you know what that means.

I have glossed over this passage several times in the process of writing this book, but recently I heard these words in my spirit: You cannot enter heaven with unforgiveness in your spirit!

Wow!

I was shocked when I heard the words, and I struggled with them, but God opened my eyes to see the following truth:

Heaven is for forgiven people. We enter heaven not by our works of righteousness but through the blood of Jesus, the blood that forgives us of our sins. "Forgiven by the blood of Jesus" is heaven's stamp over our spirit. So, if forgiveness is what grants us access into heaven, then when we fail to forgive, we shut off the access to heaven. A person with unforgiveness in his or her spirit cannot enter and enjoy heaven, the headquarters of forgiven people.

When believers know this, they will quickly forgive and walk in love. I don't want to spend eternity repaying my debt to the Father!

Repair the broken bridges in your relationships. The prophecy of Isaiah 58:12 is relevant here: "Those from among you shall build the old waste places; you shall raise up the foundations of many generations; and you shall be called the Repairer of the Breach, the Restorer of Streets to Dwell in."

Be known as the Repairer of the breach and the Restorer of streets.

Christianity is a call to restoration, not condemnation. "Brethren, if a man is overtaken in any trespass, you who *are* spiritual restore such a one in a spirit of gentleness, considering yourself lest you also be tempted" (Galatians 6:1). We should not celebrate when others fail; rather, we should pray and strengthen them. One attribute of spiritual people is their willingness to restore their fellow brother or sister who "is overtaken in any trespass." It is not about how long you pray or how many chapters of the Bible you read in a day!

The idea of "any trespass" means I do not have the right to categorise and judge the brother's sin. I should not develop a holier-than-thou attitude and scream, "How could you?" or go about saying, "Have you heard?" My duty to that fellow brother or sister, the only one sanctioned by Jesus Christ, is to "restore such a one in a spirit of gentleness."

The devil's goal is to deplete the Body of Christ because he knows that there is strength in numbers. The more he can deplete us, the more he can weaken our influence in the world. And guess what? He uses fellow ministers and believers to achieve his goal by using people's sins as sermons. As it were, we wash our dirty linen in public and the unbelievers we are trying to reach mock us as we fight with one another. Then we turn and wonder why we are ineffective in reaching the world for Jesus. While we don't condone sin and give people a license to sin, our goal towards any brother or sister who is "overtaken in any trespass" is "to restore such a one in a spirit of gentleness" and not condemn them.

I looked up the Greek word translated overtaken, and it has the connotation of being taken by surprise. So, this is not a preplanned or well-thought-out sin. A Christian, one born again with God's incorruptible Word and washed by the blood of Jesus, does not plan to sin. He is overtaken by sin. Satan springs a surprise on him or her and catches him or her unawares. When we know this, we would be gentle towards our fellow brother or sister. This is the context Paul wrote of "considering yourself lest you also be tempted." Just as the brother fell, we too can fall if we are not careful . So, spare your harsh words and forgive and restore that brother!

Jesus advised His disciples in the following way: "If you bring your gift to the altar, and there remember that your brother has something against you, leave your gift there before the altar, and go your way. First be reconciled to your brother, and then come and offer your gift" (Matthew 5:23–24).

That's the spirit of true Christianity. Your gift is not as important as your relationship with your brother!

God, our Father, is the Restorer of broken relationships. As I write this, I see God asking someone in the same way He asked Cain, "Where is Abel thy brother?"

Where is your brother, sister, friend, spouse, son, daughter?

Will you be best buddies with everyone? No. The other person might not want the relationship again, but ensure that there is no root of bitterness within you (Hebrews 12:15). The admonition is to do your best to live peaceably with all men (Romans 12:18).

Remember: "Blessed are the peacemakers, for they shall be called sons of God" (Matthew 5:9).

10

Guide and Leader

Reference in the Lord's Prayer: **"And do not lead us into temptation."**

When Jesus asked His disciples to pray, "And do not lead us into temptation", He revealed yet another hidden title of God: Our Guide and Leader.

God did not design us to go through life on our own. If that were the case, we would be at the mercy of the forces of darkness. In His infinite mercy, He is not only our Father, King, Master, and the other titles that we have explored, He is also our Guide and Leader.

One of the major animals God used to describe us is the sheep:

Isaiah 53:6
⁶ All we like SHEEP have gone astray; we have turned, every one, to his own way; and the LORD has laid on Him the iniquity of us all.

John 10:14
¹⁴ I am the good shepherd; and I know My *SHEEP,* and am known by My own.

Sheep are amazing animals, but they lack two things—a sense of direction and a sense of danger. Left alone, they will self-destruct. Similarly, if God were to leave us to our own ways, we would self-destruct. Therefore, He made Himself available as our Guide and Leader in life.

As our Guide, God shows us the way and points the direction to us; as our Leader, He goes with us along the way and ensures that we arrive at our destination.

There is no one better to lead us than Him who knows the end from the beginning (Isaiah 46:10). He is not just our God; He is our leader.

Micah 2:13 NLT
[11] Your LEADER will break out and lead you out of exile, out through the gates of the enemy cities, back to your own land. Your king will lead you; THE LORD HIMSELF WILL GUIDE YOU.

Here our God is called our Leader, Breaker, King, and Guide. He is everything we need to go through life successfully.

As our Leader and Guide, God knows all the landmines the enemy will set for our souls, and He will lead us through the right paths so we avoid them. That's why Jesus asked us to pray, "And lead us not into temptation". There are temptations that the enemy has planned to entrap us, but God will not lead us into them.

Proverbs 1:17 says, "Surely, in vain the net is spread in the sight of any bird." Whatever the enemy is planning, it is in vain if we allow God to lead us.

In Psalm 23:4, the Lord, our Shepherd, promises to lead us "in the path of righteousness for His name's sake." There is a path of righteousness or a right path, and God has covenanted to lead us on that path.

Proverbs 12:28 tells us about the path of righteousness that God promised to lead us along: "In the way of righteousness is life, and in its pathway there is no death." I like the idea that there is no death in the way of righteousness that God has promised to lead us.

God is our Leader and Guide.

Psalm 48:14
¹⁴ For this is God, Our God forever and ever; **He will be our guide even to death**.

I like this Scripture because it is a promise that even to death, until we take our last breath, our God will be our Guide and Leader.

Isaiah 48:17
¹⁷ Thus says the Lord, your Redeemer, The Holy One of Israel: "I am the Lord your God, Who teaches you to profit, Who leads you by the way you should go."

When God leads us, we profit, make progress and, become conformed to His image. But when we lead ourselves, we cannot guarantee the outcome.

In the New Testament, one of the primary roles of the Holy Spirit is to lead and guide us into all truth. "However, when He, the Spirit of truth, has come, **He will guide you into all truth**; for He will not speak on His own authority, but whatever He hears He will speak; and He will tell you things to come" (John 16:13).

10.2

How God Leads

To guide means to provide direction, instruction, and correction. And there are several ways God guides and leads us: visions, dreams, confirmation by others, and so on. However, the primary way God leads us today is through His Word by His Spirit.

God will not lead us outside His Word. Any leading that contradicts God's Word is from the devil. Even the Holy Spirit in John 16:13 "will not speak of His own authority."

If the Holy Spirit does not speak outside the authority of God's Word, run away from any revelation that you cannot find in God's Word. God's Word is heaven's constitution—the final arbiter to judge every revelation, impression, or even inner witness. The Holy Spirit will speak only of what is in God's Word. For example, God will not lead you to claim another man's husband or wife, or someone's car!

God's Word is our compass to lead us in life. Its instructions cover every area of our lives. The revealed Word of God should be used to judge every instance of leading: visions, dreams, prophetic utterances, and so on.

The next most important way God leads us is through the inward witness. The inward witness is "a knowing" or "an impression" in your spirit that you cannot explain but you know is the right thing to do. The inward witness, however, must be in line with God's Word.

Some call it the green light in your spirit, others call it a hunch, and still others call it inward peace.

Inward peace is important. If you do not have peace internally concerning any decision you want to take, then you need to stop and consider it again.

Romans 14:17
17 For the kingdom of God is not eating and drinking, but **righteousness** and **peace** and **joy** in the Holy Spirit.

Righteousness, peace, and joy in the Holy Spirit are three ways to know the leading of God in your inward man:

Righteousness: Is it right in God's sight?
Peace: Do I have peace internally with this leading?
Joy: Do I feel good about it deep within in my spirit?

If you apply these filters to every inward witness, you will know whether it is God leading you or not.

The other ways God leads include visions, dreams, the audible voice of the Spirit, confirmation from other people, and so on (see Numbers 12:6–8).

A caveat: please apply caution to visions, dreams, prophecies from others, and even the audible voice of the Spirit, as they can be counterfeited. Use the first two methods of leading—God's Word and inner witness and peace—to judge any vision, dream, or audible voice you hear.

10.3

Cooperating with God's Leading

God is our Leader and Guide, but He will not force His instructions on us: "I will instruct you and teach you in the way you should go; I will guide you with my eye. Do not be like the horse or like the mule, which have no understanding, which must be harnessed with bit and bridle, else they will not come near you" (Psalm 32:8–9).

Although God has promised to lead and guide us, He warned us not to be "like the horse or like the mule, which haave no understanding."

The horse is swift, while the mule is sluggish. The horse needs to be restrained from running too far ahead; the mule needs to be pulled to move. Both, according to God, lack understanding.

Don't be presumptuous like the horse, running ahead of God, or be stubborn like the mule, unwilling to follow God's lead.

We need to walk in step with God, to be like the sheep, listening to our Shepherd's voice and walking in line with His revealed plan (see John 10).

To cooperate with God, we need to do two things: trust and test.

By trusting, we must believe that God's plan for us is the best, even when it doesn't make sense from a human standpoint. God knows the future better than we know our past, so we must be willing to trust His leading.

Sometimes we think we know what we are supposed to do or the way to go but we feel God is leading us in another direction. Should we obey the leading? My answer is simple: trust Him. God led the Israelites by a different route although it was longer, because the shorter one would have had a lot of challenges. "Then it came to pass, when Pharaoh had let the people go, *that God did not lead them by way of the land of the Philistines, although that was near*; for God said, 'Lest perhaps the people change their minds when they see war, and return to Egypt'" (Exodus 13:17).

The second thing we need to do is test it. What do I mean? By testing, we act and review our steps. If it is God leading us, as we step out, the instruction will become clearer.

In Psalm 119:105, we see a beautiful illustration of why we need to take steps of faith. "Your word is a lamp to my feet and a light to my path."

Sometimes in our lives, we want to know the end from the beginning, so we wait for God to give us the full instructions for the journey before we set out. And we wait … and wait … and wait. While we are waiting on God, God is waiting for us.

God's Word is a lamp to our feet and a light to our path. A lamp illuminates only the immediate vicinity. On a dark path, a lamp will not show you beyond your next three to five steps; it will not show you the end from the beginning. You have two choices: to wait there and do nothing or take a step based on the light you have. If you choose to do the latter, you will find out that as you take the first step, the area of illumination will increase and the lamp will eventually illuminate your path. It soon will have become not just a lamp to your feet but also a light to your path.

That is how God works. He gives us directions as a lamp to our feet, but if we fail to take the step, He will not give us another instruction; when we act by faith and step out, that's when the lamp becomes a light unto our path.

God rarely gives us the picture of the end from the beginning. If that were the case, there would be no need for faith and waiting on Him. However, taking steps of faith is not the same as blind stupidity. Many years ago, a young man jumped into a lion's den in a zoo because he wanted to prove something—whatever that was. This is not a case of God leading someone; it's a case of blind stupidity! God will not lead you into a lion's den. God did not lead Daniel into the lion's den. God delivered him from it. That's why I say you need to test it.

We are admonished to examine all things, including every spirit, but to hold on to that which is good (1 Timothy 5:21; 1 John 4:1). Sometimes what we think is God leading us is our flesh or even a deceptive spirit. At such times, we need to repent, ask God for forgiveness, and learn from the experience.

God leads. We need to learn to trust Him to lead and guide us.

Isaiah 48:17–19
¹⁷ Thus says the Lord, your Redeemer, the Holy One of Israel: "I am the Lord your God, Who teaches you to profit, Who leads you by the way you should go.
¹⁸ Oh, that you had heeded my commandments! Then your peace would have been like a river, and your righteousness like the waves of the sea.
¹⁹ Your descendants also would have been like the sand, and the offspring of your body like the grains of sand; his name would not have been cut off nor destroyed from before Me."

11

Strong Deliverer

Reference in the Lord's Prayer: "**Deliver us from the evil one.**"

When Jesus asked His disciples to pray, "But deliver us from the evil one", He revealed yet another hidden title of God: The Strong Deliverer.

In that statement, Jesus recognized there is an evil one; but the good news is that our Father, our Strong Deliverer, will not leave us at the mercy of the wicked one. When we are hemmed in by situations and circumstances, and it looks as if there is no way of escape, our Strong Deliverer will step in and bring us out if we trust in Him.

Psalm 140:7 (NIV)
[7] Sovereign LORD, MY STRONG DELIVERER, you shield my head in the day of battle.

"My Strong Deliverer"—I like that. He would shield our heads on the day of battle.

Deliverance is when God steps in and brings you out of a helpless or nearly impossible situation. We see such an account in 1 Samuel 17:34–35. In this chapter, David describes his experience as a shepherd to Saul. He notes that "when a lion or bear came and took a lamb out of the flock, I went out after it and struck it, and *delivered the lamb from its mouth.*"

Deliverance is nothing short of a miracle. When the lion was about to devour the prey, a helpless lamb, David struck it and delivered the lamb from its mouth.

Deliverance is usually necessary when you have a powerful foe whose intent is to destroy you and there is nothing you can do about it. A lamb is utterly helpless before a lion unless an external force or person acts on its behalf.

This is the picture of our deliverance. We are helpless before the enemy, but God did not give our soul to him to devour us.

One of the reasons God gave Jesus up for us is to deliver us from this present evil world (Galatians 1:4). As it were, we are like the sheep here, and the devil like the lion or bear, and Jesus like David. When Jesus saw that the devil had taken us captive, He went after the devil, bruised his head and delivered us from the captivity of sin (Genesis 3:15; Colossians 2:15; Luke 11:21–22). And today, when the devil comes in like a roaring lion looking for whom he may devour, God still does not leave us at his mercy. He goes after the devil to deliver us from his clutches.

Because God is our Strong Deliverer, we will not be defeated. Our heads will not be covered with shame. He is the One who fights for us.

Isaiah 49:25

25 But thus says the LORD: "Even the captives of the mighty shall be taken away, and the prey of the terrible be delivered; for **I will contend with him who contends with you, and I will save your children.**"

God has covenanted to contend with those who contend with us and save us and our children. Isn't that wonderful?

The captives of the mighty and the prey of the terrible shall be delivered. Praise the Lord!

Psalm 124 is a beautiful psalm of deliverance:

¹ "If it had not been the Lord who was on our side," Let Israel now say—

² "If it had not been the Lord Who was on our side, when men rose up against us,

³ Then they would have swallowed us alive, when their wrath was kindled against us;

⁴ Then the waters would have overwhelmed us, the stream would have gone over our soul;

⁵ Then the swollen waters would have gone over our soul."

⁶ Blessed be the Lord, who has not given us as prey to their teeth.

⁷ Our soul has escaped as a bird from the snare of the fowlers; the snare is broken, and we have escaped.

⁸ Our help is in the name of the Lord, Who made heaven and earth.

Our Strong Deliverer will deliver us from wicked men, dangerous situations, and the devil!

11.2

Four Accounts of Deliverance

There are so many examples of God delivering people from difficult and nearly impossible situations in the Bible, but we will consider only four here:

1. Hezekiah and Judah (2 Chronicles 32)

In this chapter, we see Hezekiah besieged by Sennacherib, the king of Assyria, and his army. Sennacherib, at that time, was the most powerful king in the world. He came against Judah, but Hezekiah refused to cave in, trusting in God to deliver him and his people. Sennacherib became very angry and very boastful. He said three important things to Hezekiah and his people:

He advised them not to die for nothing: "Thus says Sennacherib, king of Assyria: 'In what do you trust, that you remain under siege in Jerusalem? *Does not Hezekiah persuade you to give yourselves over to die by famine and by thirst*, saying, "The Lord our God will deliver us from the hand of the king of Assyria"?'" (vv. 10–11).

He compared God with the other gods: "Do you not know what I and my fathers have done to all the peoples of other lands? Were the gods of the nations of those lands in any way able to deliver their lands out of my hand? Who was there among all the gods of those nations that my fathers utterly destroyed that could deliver his people from my hand, that your God should be able to deliver you from my hand?" (vv. 13–14)

He concluded that not even God would be able to deliver Hezekiah and Judah from his hand. "Now therefore, do not let Hezekiah deceive you or persuade you like this, and do not believe him; for no god of any nation or kingdom was able to deliver his people from my hand or the hand of my fathers. How much less will your God deliver you from my hand?'" (v. 15)

How did the story end?

2 Chronicles 32:20–22

[20] Now because of this King Hezekiah and the prophet Isaiah, the son of Amoz, prayed and cried out to heaven.

[21] THEN THE LORD SENT AN ANGEL who cut down every mighty man of valour, leader, and captain in the camp of the king of Assyria. So he returned shamefaced to his own land. And when he had gone into the temple of his god, some of his own offspring struck him down with the sword there.

[22] THUS THE LORD SAVED HEZEKIAH and the inhabitants of Jerusalem from the hand of Sennacherib the king of Assyria, and from the hand of all others, AND GUIDED THEM ON EVERY SIDE.

Did you notice that the words "saved" and "guided" are used to denote the deliverance they experienced? Hidden in the word "salvation" are guidance and deliverance. Enjoy all the blessings of your salvation.

2. Shadrach, Meshach, and Abed-Nego (Daniel 3)

No account of deliverance would be complete without mentioning the account of the three Hebrew boys in Daniel 3. Nebuchadnezzar, the king of Babylon, in his vainglory, built a statue of gold of himself and instructed everyone to bow before it. Daniel's three friends refused, and the king convulsed in rage and threatened to cast them into the midst of a burning fiery furnace.

What was the response of Shadrach, Meshach, and Abed-Nego in Daniel 3:16–18?

> Daniel 3:16–18
> ¹⁶ Shadrach, Meshach, and Abed-Nego answered and said to the king, "O Nebuchadnezzar, we have no need to answer you in this matter.
> ¹⁷ If that is the case, OUR GOD WHOM WE SERVE IS ABLE TO DELIVER US from the burning fiery furnace, AND HE WILL DELIVER US FROM YOUR HAND, O king.
> ¹⁸ But if not, let it be known to you, O king, that we do not serve your gods, nor will we worship the gold image which you have set up."

So confident were they in God's ability to deliver them that they told the king, "We have no need to answer you in this matter."

What confidence! They knew God was able to, and would, deliver them. What a bold statement.

"God ... is able to deliver us" deals with His ability.

"He will deliver us" deals with His willingness.

They knew God's ability and willingness to deliver them. And God delivered them from the burning fiery furnace. God can and will also deliver us from the fiery furnace.

3. Daniel (Daniel 6)

Daniel's compatriots in the government, filled with demonic hatred, conspired against him, and he was thrown into the lions' den because of his refusal to pray to the king. God sent an angel and shut up the lions' mouths and delivered Daniel.

Daniel 6:19–22

¹⁹ Then the king arose very early in the morning and went in haste to the den of lions.

²⁰ And when he came to the den, he cried out with a lamenting voice to Daniel. The king spoke, saying to Daniel, "Daniel, servant of the living God, has your God, whom you serve continually, been able to deliver you from the lions?"

²¹ Then Daniel said to the king, "O king, live forever!

²² MY GOD SENT HIS ANGEL AND SHUT THE LIONS' MOUTHS, so that they have not hurt me, because I was found innocent before Him; and also, O king, I have done no wrong before you."

4. Peter (Acts 12)

The fourth and final example is seen in Acts 12:11. Peter had a death sentence over his life and was waiting for his execution, but the church prayed, and God sent His angel to deliver him.

Acts 12:11

¹¹ And when Peter had come to himself, he said, "Now I know for certain that the Lord has sent His angel, and HAS DELIVERED ME FROM THE HAND OF HEROD and from all the expectation of the Jewish people."

God is our Strong Deliverer. Are you hemmed in like Hezekiah? Do you have a death sentence over your life like Peter? Are they plotting to throw you into the fiery furnace like Daniel's three friends or into the lion's den like Daniel himself? Look to our God, the Strong Deliverer, for He is able to deliver you, and He will deliver you.

Paul said of God in 2 Timothy 4:18, "And the Lord will deliver me from every evil work and preserve me for His heavenly kingdom. To Him be glory forever and ever. Amen!"

I confess like Paul that the Lord will deliver me from every evil work and preserve me for His heavenly kingdom in Jesus' name. Make it your confession.

12

Our Protector

Reference in the Lord's Prayer: **"Deliver us from the evil one."**

When Jesus asked His disciples to pray, "But deliver us from the evil one", He revealed yet another hidden title of God: Our Protector.

While deliverance deals with God bringing us out of a difficult or impossible situation, protection deals with God preventing the attacks of the enemy.

God is our protector. As we noted in the last chapter, one of the reasons Jesus gave Himself up for us is to deliver us from the evil one. "Who gave Himself for our sins, that *He might deliver us from this present evil age*, according to the will of our God and Father" (Galatians 1:4).

This verse recognizes that our present age is evil but thank God we are not just people saved from sins; we are also people with God's protection against satanic attacks. Our Saviour is also our Strong Deliverer and Protector! When we call the name Jesus, we call on salvation, healing, provision, deliverance, and all.

Proverbs 18:10
[10] The name of the LORD is A STRONG TOWER; the righteous run to it and are safe.

The name of Jesus is a strong tower of protection. The righteous—saved people—"run to it and are safe" and protected.

Use the name. It's the name of protection. There is a covenant of protection for you. Psalm 121:7–8 says, "The Lord shall preserve you from all evil; He shall preserve your soul. The Lord shall preserve your going out and your coming in from this time forth, and even forevermore."

There are many words used to describe our protection by Jehovah: "refuge", "shield", "pavilion", "strong tower", "rock", "fortress", "hiding place", "high tower", and so on.

Refuge: Psalm 46:1–3
¹ GOD IS OUR REFUGE and strength, a very present help in trouble. ² Therefore we will not fear, even though the earth be removed, and though the mountains be carried into the midst of the sea; ³ Though its waters roar and be troubled, though the mountains shake with its swelling. Selah

Pavilion: Psalm 27:5
⁵ For in the time of trouble He shall hide me IN HIS PAVILION; in the secret place of His tabernacle He shall hide me; He shall set me high upon a rock.

Hiding Place: Psalm 32:7
⁵ YOU ARE MY HIDING PLACE; You shall preserve me from trouble; You shall surround me with songs of deliverance.

Shelter and Shade: Isaiah 25:4 NIV
⁴ You have been a refuge for the poor, a refuge for the needy in their distress, a SHELTER from the storm and a SHADE from the heat …

12.2

Psalm 91: A Covenant of Protection

So important is this aspect of protection that a whole psalm was dedicated to it—Psalm 91. While Psalm 124 is God's covenant of deliverance, Psalm 91 is the covenant of protection. It is a comprehensive protection cover over your life. I want you to carefully study it, meditate on it, and make it your daily confession.

God, Our Secret Place, Refuge, and Fortress (vv. 1–2)

¹ He who dwells in THE SECRET PLACE of the Most High shall abide under the shadow of the Almighty.
² I will say of the Lord, "He is MY REFUGE and MY FORTRESS; My God, in Him I will trust."

Dwelling in God's secret place is living in the consciousness of His divine presence. It is going out every day in the consciousness that Jehovah is with you and for you as you go out.

One key to activating the divine presence is through your confession. Notice that in the second verse, the psalmist confessed, "I will say of the Lord, 'He is MY REFUGE and MY FORTRESS; My God, in Him I will trust.' " What we say of God is critical. We release God into our day through our confession. What is your confession of the Lord today?

God, Our Deliverer, Covering, Shield, and Buckler (vv. 3–4)

³ Surely HE SHALL DELIVER you from the snare of the fowler and from the perilous pestilence.
⁴ He shall COVER YOU with His feathers, and under His wings you shall take refuge; His truth shall be your SHIELD AND BUCKLER.

The third verse gives us the divine guarantee that God will deliver us. It begins with *surely*, an unshakeable confidence borne out of an encounter with God and an experience of God's previous deliverance.

What will God deliver us from? Two things: (1) *from the snare of the fowler*. This deals with deliverance from the entrapments of the enemy of our soul which we have covered in the previous chapter; (2) *from the perilous pestilence*. The Hebrew word translated perilous is *havvah*, and according to the notes in my Dakes Annotated Reference Bible is defined as a *rushing calamity; one that sweeps everything before it*. Wow! The word pestilence is the word *deber* which is also translated plague. So, the perilous pestilence is a rushing plague, one that destroys everything along its path. Would coronavirus fall into this category? Perhaps, yes. But the good news is that there is an assurance from God that He will deliver us from the perilous pestilence.

God, Our Defence from Every Evil (vv. 5–8)

5 You shall not be afraid of the terror by night, nor of the arrow that flies by day,
6 Nor of the pestilence that walks in darkness, nor of the destruction that lays waste at noonday.
7 A thousand may fall at your side, and ten thousand at your right hand; BUT IT SHALL NOT COME NEAR YOU.
8 Only with your eyes shall you look, and see the reward of the wicked.

The protection covers night, day, darkness and light. Some people are afraid of the night or the dark, diagnosed as nyctophobia. Psalm 91 is a cure for nyctophobia. Whether by day or by night, we are protected.

"It shall not come near you" is such a powerful promise. We need to stand in faith and tell the enemy of our soul, "You shall not come near me and my household in Jesus' name."

God, Our Dwelling Place and Protection (vv. 9–10)

⁹ Because you have made the LORD, who is my refuge, even the Most High, YOUR DWELLING PLACE,
¹⁰ NO EVIL SHALL BEFALL YOU, nor shall any plague come near your dwelling;

It gets even better here. Because God is our dwelling place, no evil shall befall us. Whatever is defined as evil shall not befall us. One person who experienced this was Solomon. He said in 1 Kings 5:4, "But now the LORD my God has given me rest on every side; *there is* neither adversary nor evil occurrence." I claim this promise also—rest on every side! No adversary or evil occurrence.

Angelic Cover (vv. 11–12)

¹¹ For He shall give His angels charge over you, to keep you in all your ways.
¹² In their hands they shall bear you up, lest you dash your foot against a stone.

We are not defenseless. We have the angels of God covering us.

Did you notice that the reason why no evil will befall us nor shall any plague come near our dwelling places is because of the ministry of angels?

¹⁰ No evil shall befall you, nor shall any plague come near your dwelling;

¹¹ FOR HE SHALL GIVE HIS ANGELS CHARGE OVER YOU, to keep you in all your ways.

We need to continually remind ourselves of our angelic cover by saying, "Father, I thank You for the angels you have given charge over me. Thank You because your angels surround me; Your angels guard me as I go out today."

One missing aspect of the New Covenant for many Christians is the role of angels. There is a lot of confusion about who they are and what their roles are in the lives of believers. Some have relegated it to the Old Testament saying that since we have the Holy Spirit we do not need them. But reading through the New Testament, one would be amazed to see that angels played crucial roles in the lives of God's people:

an angel foretold the birth of Jesus (Luke 1:26–37),
another angel told Joseph to take Jesus to Egypt (Matthew 2:13–15),
angels ministered to Jesus in the wilderness (Matthew 4:13),
an angel strengthened Jesus in prayer (Luke 22:43),
another angel rolled away the stone on the resurrection morning (Matthew 28:2),
an angel brought Peter out of prison (Acts 12:7–12),
an angel sent Philip to Gaza to minister to the Ethiopian eunuch (Acts 8:26),
an angel saved Paul from the shipwreck (Acts 27:23–24), and
another angel gave John the revelation of the book of Revelation (Revelation 1:1).

We could go on about the ministry of angels in the New Testament. I think that because some have run off to the ditch concerning angels, a lot of believers have not appreciated their roles. They are our supernatural helpers sent forth to minister for us (Hebrews 1:14).

Pray with me: "Father, thank you for my angelic helpers. I receive their ministry today in my life and over my family, work and ministry in Jesus name."

Victory Over Satanic Forces (vv. 13)

¹³ You shall tread upon the lion and the cobra, the young lion and the serpent you shall trample underfoot.

We are victorious people. Luke 10:19, "Behold, I give you the authority to trample on serpents and scorpions, and over all the power of the enemy, and nothing shall by any means hurt you."

Salvation, Honour, Life (vv. 14–16)

¹⁴ Because he has set his love upon Me, therefore I will deliver him; I will set him on high, because he has known My name.
¹⁵ He shall call upon Me, and I will answer him; I will be with him in trouble; I will deliver him and honour him.
¹⁶ With long life I will satisfy him, and show him My salvation."

Psalm 91 begins with an exaltation from the psalmist. In the last three verses, we see God speaking, repeating everything the psalmist has said about our deliverance but also adding honour and long life.

Long life is your inheritance. Your life shall not be cut short in Jesus name. And as you live long, your life will be marked with honour and not disgrace, shame or reproach in Jesus name.

13

The All-Powerful God

Reference in the Lord's Prayer: "**For Yours is the ... power.**"

When Jesus asked His disciples to pray, "For Yours is the ... power", He revealed another hidden title of God: The All-Powerful or Omnipotent God!

The idea of God's omnipotence runs throughout the Scriptures. Genesis 1:1 opens the account of God's omnipotence, the God who created the heavens and earth out of nothing. We also see God's omnipotence in Psalm 62:11, "God has spoken once, twice I have heard this: that power belongs to God."

Power belongs to God! This is a concept we need to settle forever in our hearts.

God's Power Is Absolute

Job 9:12
¹² If He takes away, who can hinder Him? WHO CAN SAY TO HIM, "WHAT ARE YOU DOING?"

2 Chronicles 20:6
⁶ O Lord God of our fathers, are You not God in heaven, and do You not rule over all the kingdoms of the nations, and in Your hand is there not power and might, SO THAT NO ONE IS ABLE TO WITHSTAND YOU?

God's Power Is Over All Creation

Job 26:7–14
⁷ He stretches out the north over empty space; HE HANGS THE EARTH ON NOTHING.

⁸ He binds up the water in his thick clouds, yet the clouds are not broken under it.

⁹ He covers the face of His throne, and spreads His cloud over it.

¹⁰ He drew a circular horizon on the face of the waters, at the boundary of light and darkness.

¹¹ The pillars of heaven tremble, and are astonished at His rebuke.

¹² He stirs up the sea with His power, and by His understanding He breaks up the storm.

¹³ By His Spirit He adorned the heavens; His hand pierced the fleeing serpent.

¹⁴ Indeed these are the mere edges of His ways, and how small a whisper we hear of Him! But the thunder of His power who can understand?"

God's Power Knows No Limitations

Jeremiah 32:17, 27
¹⁷ Ah, Lord GOD! Behold, You have made the heavens and the earth by Your great power and outstretched arm. THERE IS NOTHING TOO HARD FOR YOU ...

²⁷ Behold, I am the LORD, the God of all flesh. IS THERE ANYTHING TOO HARD FOR ME?

Luke 1:37
³⁷ For with God nothing will be impossible.

God is the All-Powerful One. He is the Monarch of the Universe, the Sovereign Lord, the Mighty God, and the Almighty. All these titles point to one thing—God's omnipotence. He is the Blessed and Only Potentate (1 Timothy 6:15), the One with absolute authority in heaven and on earth (Matthew 28:18).

We serve the All-Powerful One. When a man cannot reproduce, he is termed impotent. But not God. He is the Omnipotent One. "Omni" means "all" or "unlimited". Our Father is the Unlimited God, the God with unlimited power. He has never failed to reproduce His will, counsel, and purposes in every generation and in any situation.

Isaiah 55:11
[11] So shall My word be that goes forth from My mouth; it shall not return to Me void, but it shall accomplish what I please, and it shall prosper in the thing for which I sent it.

Two words associated with God's Word based on this verse are "accomplish" and "prosper" (or "accomplishment" and "prosperity"). Embedded in every one of God's Words is the power to reproduce—to bring to pass what God wants. It is an impossibility for God's Word to return to Him void—empty or frustrated.

God's Word is likened to the rain in this passage. Isaiah 55:10–11 says, "For as the rain comes down, and the snow from heaven, and do not return there, but water the earth, and make it bring forth and bud, that it may give seed to the sower and bread to the eater, so shall My Word be …"

There is one thing we are certain about regarding the rain: nothing can stop it, once it starts to fall, from touching the earth. It must reach the earth. In the same manner, God says that nothing can stop His Word from coming to pass. It is impossible! If you cannot stop the rain from coming down and watering the earth, you cannot prevent the Word of God from accomplishing its purpose.

When Abram made the mistake that brought Ishmael, God came to him and said to him, "I am Almighty God; walk before me and be blameless" (Genesis 17:1).

God literally told Abram, "The reason you failed is because you do not know who I am. I am Almighty God; I bring to pass every promise of Mine. Nothing is too hard for Me to do!"

We, too, like Abram, need to walk in the consciousness of who this great God is.

When God delivered the Israelites from Pharaoh's hand in Egypt, Moses composed a song about the greatness of God's power in the fifteenth chapter of the book of Exodus, in which he celebrated God's omnipotence.

Exodus 15:1–7

¹ Then Moses and the children of Israel sang this song to the LORD, and spoke, saying: "I will sing to the LORD, FOR HE HAS TRIUMPHED GLORIOUSLY! **The horse and its rider He has thrown into the sea**!

² **The LORD is my strength and song**, and He has become my salvation; He is my God, and I will praise Him; My father's God, and I will exalt Him.

³ **The LORD is a man of war**; The LORD is His name.
⁴ Pharaoh's chariots and his army He has cast into the sea; his chosen captains also are drowned in the Red Sea.

⁵ The depths have covered them; they sank to the bottom like a stone.

⁶ **Your right hand, O LORD, has become glorious in power; Your right hand, O LORD, has dashed the enemy in pieces**.

⁷ And in the greatness of Your excellence You have overthrown those who rose against You; You sent forth Your wrath; it consumed them like stubble."

We serve the All-Powerful Being, the Almighty. He triumphs gloriously over anyone who rises up against Him.

To Him belongs power forever.

13.2

All Power Comes from God

Sometimes people in positions of authority are blindsided by the power in such positions and think that they are very powerful. Perish the thought! All power or authority comes from God.

Romans 13:1
¹ Let every soul be subject to the governing authorities. FOR THERE IS NO AUTHORITY EXCEPT FROM GOD, and the authorities that exist are appointed by God.

There is no authority except from God! God is the ultimate source of every authority, and any authority that we exert on earth is simply a delegated authority from God.

When God made man and gave him dominion over the earth, He revealed that He is the source of man's authority. Any authority we exert on earth is from Him and should be used for His purposes and His glory alone and is not to be used to oppress others. We are simply stewards of God's authority as leaders.

Did you notice that God did not give man dominion over man? He said, "Let them [male and female] have dominion over the fish of the seas, over the birds of the air and over every creeping thing that creeps on the earth" (Genesis 1:26). Man's original dominion did not include human beings. We are not meant to dominate each other; we are meant to inspire and influence each other towards godliness and greatness!

When we fail to understand this concept of power and authority, we become like Pilate, who felt that he had the power to crucify or release Jesus. He felt that the destiny of Jesus was in his hands.

He asked Jesus whether He was the Son of God, and when Jesus refused to answer him, he said to Jesus, "Are You not speaking to me? Do You not know that I have power to crucify You, and power to release You?" (John 19:10).

Sometimes we, too, are like Pilate; our positions blindside us, and we attribute to ourselves power we do not have. We think we have it in our hands to determine people's futures. But how mistaken we are.

What was Jesus' response to Pilate? "Jesus answered, 'You could have no power at all against me unless it had been given you from above. Therefore the one who delivered me to you has the greater sin'" (John 19:11).

Jesus reminded Pilate that he had no power over him except the one given to him from above. We need to walk in the consciousness of this revelation. No man on earth has any power over you, and any power a man may exert has been given to him from above. And we can remove that power over us not by fighting them but by praying to God our Father to remove that authority if they are misusing it.

Daniel 4:17
[17] This decision is by the decree of the watchers, and the sentence by the word of the holy ones, in order that the living may know that THE MOST HIGH RULES IN THE KINGDOM OF MEN, GIVES IT TO WHOMEVER HE WILL, and sets over it the lowest of men.

The lesson is important. Authority is spiritual. And our God is the source of every authority.

Did you notice that in Jesus' response to Pilate, He immediately connected power and sin?

John 19:11
¹¹ Jesus answered, "You could have no power at all against Me unless it had been given you from above. THEREFORE THE ONE WHO DELIVERED ME TO YOU HAS THE GREATER SIN."

What is the connection between authority and sin? Every abuse of power or authority is a sin against God that we must give an account of. The greater sin was Judas's. He abused the authority given to him as an apostle of Jesus by betraying Jesus. Pilate had a lesser sin. He knew the right thing to do, but to please the people he gave Jesus up to be crucified. Jesus told him in advance that he would give account of it before God.

Every time we abuse the power God has placed in our hands as a husband to a wife and vice versa, a parent to children, a pastor to congregants, a leader to constituents, a teacher to students, or a caregiver to patients, we sin against God, and we will give an account of it on the judgement day.

What, then, should be our attitude towards the authority we have been given?

Paul answered this question with two verses in his letter to the Corinthians.

2 Corinthians 10:8
⁸ For even if I should boast somewhat more about OUR AUTHORITY, WHICH THE LORD GAVE US FOR EDIFICATION and not for your destruction …

2 Corinthians 13:10

¹⁰ Therefore I write these things being absent, lest being present I should use sharpness, according to THE AUTHORITY WHICH THE LORD HAS GIVEN ME FOR EDIFICATION and not for destruction.

The purpose of power or authority is to edify or build people up, not to destroy, intimidate, or harass them. Remember: if we abuse our authority, we will give an account of it before God.

Just as those who abuse authority will give an account of it, those who do not respect authority will also give account to God.

Romans 13:1–2

¹ Let every soul be subject to the governing authorities. For there is no authority except from God, and the authorities that exist are appointed by God.
² Therefore whoever resists the authority resists the ordinance of God, and those who resist will bring judgment on themselves.

We bring judgement upon ourselves when we resist authority. Obey those in authority over you. Understand that it is God who has placed them there for now.

Hebrews 13:17 combines the two admonitions—for those in authority and those under authority: "Obey those who rule over you, and be submissive, for they watch out for your souls, as those who must give account. Let them do so with joy and not with grief, for that would be unprofitable for you."

Those under authority—obey; those in authority—be accountable.

14

The Glorious God

Reference in the Lord's Prayer: **"For Yours is the … glory."**

When Jesus asked His disciples to pray, "For Yours is the power and the glory", He revealed another hidden title of God: The Glorious God, or the God of Glory!

The theme of the glory of God runs throughout the Bible. For example:

Psalm 8:1
¹ O Lord, our Lord, How excellent is Your name in all the earth, Who have set YOUR GLORY above the heavens!

PSALM 24:7–8
⁷ Lift up your heads, O you gates! And be lifted up, you everlasting doors! And the KING OF GLORY shall come in.
⁸ Who is this KING OF GLORY? The Lord strong and mighty, the Lord mighty in battle.

So important is the concept of God's glory that God said He would not share His glory with another (Isaiah 42:8).

Just as God is the only and All-Powerful God, He is also the only Glorious One. Everything about Him radiates glory, beauty, elegance, splendour, and magnificence.

As a simple definition, God's glory is simply God's manifested beauty seen in or through His attributes. Glory is the signature of God upon creation. It deals with God's magnificence, splendour, opulence, greatness, acts, and all His attributes.

Usually, every time God's glory is mentioned, it is in connection with one of God's attributes:

Exodus 15:11
¹¹ Who is like You, O LORD, among the gods? Who is like You, GLORIOUS IN HOLINESS, Fearful in praises, doing wonders?

Isaiah 6:3
³ And one cried to another and said: "HOLY, HOLY, HOLY is the LORD of hosts; the whole earth is FULL OF HIS GLORY!"

In both verses above, God's glory is connected to His holiness, an attribute of God.

When Moses prayed to God desiring to see His glory, God said, "I will make all my goodness pass before you, and I will proclaim the name of the Lord before you. I will be gracious to whom I will be gracious, and I will have compassion on whom I will have compassion" (Exodus 33:18–19).

Then God fulfilled his request, as recorded in Exodus 34:6–7:

⁶ And the LORD passed before him and proclaimed, "The LORD, the LORD God, merciful and gracious, longsuffering, and abounding in goodness and truth,

⁷ Keeping mercy for thousands, forgiving iniquity and transgression and sin, by no means clearing the guilty, visiting the iniquity of the fathers upon the children and the children's children to the third and the fourth generation."

When God revealed His glory to Moses, He showed His glory in His attributes: "merciful, gracious, longsuffering, and abounding in goodness and truth."

Glory is the tangible manifestation of the person of God, usually through one of His attributes.

If glory is the tangible manifestation of the person of God, then Jesus is the embodiment of God's glory.

John 1:14
[14] And the Word became flesh and dwelt among us, and WE BEHELD HIS GLORY, the glory as of the only begotten of the Father, FULL OF GRACE AND TRUTH.

Hebrews 1:3
[3] WHO BEING THE BRIGHTNESS OF *HIS* GLORY and the express image of His person, and upholding all things by the word of His power, when He had by Himself purged our sins, sat down at the right hand of the Majesty on high.

Jesus is God's glory manifested in the flesh. The Shekinah Glory of the Old Testament tabernacled among us in the New Testament in the person of Jesus.

14.2

Power and Glory: Two Sides of the Same Coin

When Jesus asked them to pray, "For Yours is the kingdom and the power and the glory", He revealed another fundamental truth: power and glory are usually inseparable. They are two sides of the same coin.

Every kingdom is known by two things: power and glory. The devil understood this concept, because in his temptation to Jesus, he talked about both concepts.

Luke 4:5–6
⁵ Then the devil, taking Him up on a high mountain, showed Him all THE KINGDOMS of the world in a moment of time.
⁶ And the devil said to Him, "All this AUTHORITY I will give You, and their GLORY; for this has been delivered to me, and I give it to whomever I wish.

Power or authority and glory always go together. Power is usually the conveyor of glory, or glory is the end result of power. What do I mean? When Jesus turned water into wine (power), He manifested His glory (John 2:1–11). In this example, power is the conveyor of glory.

What is the lesson here? If glory is the end result of power, God demands that we give glory to His name for every manifestation of power that we experience.

Psalm 19:1
¹ The heavens declare THE GLORY OF GOD; and the firmament shows HIS HANDIWORK.

The heavens (a product of God's power) declare the glory of God. We, too, need to declare God's glory for every answer to prayer we see. We have prayed for protection, provision, healing, deliverance and so on, and God, in His infinite power has responded; we need not take it for granted. God's power in action requires us to give glory to His name (Psalm 29:2).

Give God the glory due His name. Don't ascribe your results to your skilfulness or connections or intelligence. Had God not stepped in, you would have perished in the dungeon, "for the race is not to the swift, nor the battle to the strong" (Ecclesiastes 9:11).

The account of the ten lepers comes to mind here (Luke 17:11–19). Ten lepers were cleansed, but only one came back to give glory to God. What was Jesus' response?

Luke 17:17–19
¹⁷ So Jesus answered and said, "Were there not ten cleansed? BUT WHERE ARE THE NINE?
¹⁸ Were there not any found WHO RETURNED TO GIVE GLORY TO GOD except this foreigner?"
¹⁹ And He said to him, "Arise, go your way. Your faith has made you well."

He returned to give glory for the tangible demonstration of God's power in his healing. I believe the Master's heart would have been disappointed with the other nine.

Don't forget to return to give glory to His name. Don't become so busy that you forget to give glory to God.

When David gave glory to God for choosing him as king over Israel, Michal, his wife, despised Him, and she became barren (2 Samuel 6:16–23). Don't become spiritually barren; give God the glory due to Him!

Don't become like Nebuchadnezzar in attitude, who thought that Babylon was built by the strength of his military wisdom and might:

Daniel 4:28–32

[28] All this came upon King Nebuchadnezzar.

[29] At the end of the twelve months he was walking about the royal palace of Babylon.

[30] The king spoke, saying, *"Is not this great Babylon, that I have built for a royal dwelling by my mighty power and for the honor of my majesty?"*

[31] While the word was still in the king's mouth, a voice fell from heaven: "King Nebuchadnezzar, to you it is spoken: *the kingdom has departed from you!*

[32] And they shall drive you from men, and your dwelling shall be with the beasts of the field. They shall make you eat grass like oxen; and seven times shall pass over you, *until you know that the Most High rules in the kingdom of men, and gives it to whomever He chooses."*

God humbled him. He lost his kingdom until he learnt the lesson of gratitude. No matter the kingdom you have, if God did not help you, you would not have built it.

Give the glory due to His name.

Jude 1:24–25

[24] Now to Him who is able to keep you from stumbling, and to present you faultless before the presence of His glory with exceeding joy,

[25] To God our Saviour, Who alone is wise, BE GLORY AND MAJESTY, dominion and power both now and forever. Amen.

15

The Eternal God

*Reference in the Lord's Prayer: "... **forever** ... **Amen**."*

Wow! We have reached the end of the prayer that Jesus taught His disciples. I hope you have been blessed by the insights you have received so far, just as I have been blessed writing this book.

When Jesus ended the prayer with "forever ... amen", He revealed another hidden title of God: The Eternal God!

This is perhaps the foundation of the person of God: the eternally existent One, the God whose existence cannot be traced—the self-existent One, who has no origin, source, beginning, or ending.

This is the foundation for understanding the person of God. God exists. He has no source, origin, or beginning, and therefore no end. Our finite minds cannot comprehend it. As children, we asked, "Where did God come from? Where was God before the creations of the heavens and the earth?" Do you know why we ask such questions? Our finite minds believe in the origin of things. For something to make sense, it must have a beginning. But this is not so with God. He has no beginning. Origin is alien to God, just as sin or impossibility cannot be associated with Him.

The following verses attest to the eternity of God.

Genesis 21:33
³³ Then Abraham planted a tamarisk tree in Beersheba, and there called on the name of the Lord, THE EVERLASTING GOD.

Deuteronomy 32:27
²⁷ THE ETERNAL GOD is your refuge, and underneath are THE EVERLASTING ARMS...

Psalm 90:2,
² Before the mountains were brought forth, or ever You had formed the earth and the world, EVEN FROM EVERLASTING TO EVERLASTING, YOU ARE GOD.

Isaiah 40:28
²⁸ Have you not known? Have you not heard? THE EVERLASTING GOD, the Lord, the Creator of the ends of the earth, neither faints nor is weary. His understanding is unsearchable.

Micah 5:2
² But you, Bethlehem Ephrathah, though you are little among the thousands of Judah, yet out of you shall come forth to Me the One to be Ruler in Israel, WHOSE GOINGS FORTH ARE FROM OF OLD, FROM EVERLASTING.

God is the Everlasting God. He lives in eternity, outside the boundaries of time, and therefore will live forever and ever, amen!
His kingdom is forever. Amen.
His power is forever. Amen.
His glory is forever. Amen.

"To God our Saviour, who alone is wise, be glory and majesty, dominion and power both now and forever. Amen" (Jude 1:25).

About the Author

Dr Maxwell Ubah is an apostolic-teacher whose call is to reveal the redemptive mandate of God in Christ Jesus. A product of grace, Dr Ubah is a medical doctor and a graduate of the London Business School's Sloan Fellows programme in leadership and strategy. He is the pastor of The Leadership Church, House of Rest International.

He is a leadership coach and an organizational transformation consultant to many organizations in Nigeria and across Africa.

Dr Ubah has written and published the following books:

The Amazing Scandals of Grace
A Yes God: God's Heart Concerning Your Needs
Amazing—He Loved Me This Much (an exposition on John 3:16—free e-book)

Leadership and Personal Effectiveness Books

Seven Great Life Lessons: *Powerful Strategies for Reaching Your Goals*
The Difference—What Successful People Know and Do That Ordinary People Do Not
The Alphabet of Leadership: *The A–Z of Improving Your Leadership Effectiveness*
The 5 Fundamental Principles of Work—Lessons from the Garden of Eden

Reach out to ask Dr Maxwell Ubah to speak to your team:
Twitter or Instagram: @maxwellubah
SMS: +234(0) 802 323 3321
Email: maxubah@gmail.com.

www.ingramcontent.com/pod-product-compliance
Lightning Source LLC
LaVergne TN
LVHW011708060526
838200LV00051B/2815